Global Warming

THE LUCENT LIBRARY OF SCIENCE AND TECHNOLOGY

Global Warming

by Peggy J. Parks

LUCENT
BOOKS®

THOMSON

San Diego • Detroit • New York • Sa... Waterville, Maine • London • Munich

On cover: A satellite map shows the hole in the ozone layer (pink and violet areas) over the continent of Antarctica (outlined in white).

LIBRARY OF CONGRESS CATALOGING-IN-PUBLICATION DATA

Parks, Peggy J., 1951–
   Global warming / by Peggy J. Parks.
     p. cm. — (The Lucent library of science and technology)
Summary: Discusses scientific evidence that indicates Earth's temperature is increasing and the consequences of that warming trend to life, agriculture, and lands.
Includes bibliographical references and index.
   ISBN 1-59018-319-3 (hardback : alk. paper)
   1. Global warming—Juvenile literature. [1. Global warming. 2. Climatic changes. 3. Climatology.] I. Title. II. Series.
   QC981.8.G56P35 2004b
   363. 738'74—dc22

                                                   2003012160

Table of Contents

Foreword

"The world has changed far more in the past 100 years than in any other century in history. The reason is not political or economic, but technological—technologies that flowed directly from advances in basic science."

— Stephen Hawking, "A Brief History of Relativity," *Time,* 2000

The twentieth-century scientific and technological revolution that British physicist Stephen Hawking describes in the above quote has transformed virtually every aspect of human life at an unprecedented pace. Inventions unimaginable a century ago have not only become commonplace but are now considered necessities of daily life. As science historian James Burke writes, "We live surrounded by objects and systems that we take for granted, but which profoundly affect the way we behave, think, work, play, and in general conduct our lives."

For example, in just one hundred years, transportation systems have dramatically changed. In 1900 the first gasoline-powered motorcar had just been introduced, and only 144 miles of U.S. roads were hard-surfaced. Horse-drawn trolleys still filled the streets of American cities. The airplane had yet to be invented. Today 217 million vehicles speed along 4 million miles of U.S. roads. Humans have flown to the moon and commercial aircraft are capable of transporting passengers across the Atlantic Ocean in less than three hours.

The transformation of communications has been just as dramatic. In 1900 most Americans lived and worked on farms without electricity or mail delivery. Few people had ever heard a radio or spoken on a telephone. A hundred years later, 98 percent of American homes have telephones and televisions and more than 50 percent have personal computers. Some families even have more than one television and computer, and cell phones are now commonplace, even among the young. Data beamed from communication satellites routinely predict global weather conditions and fiber-optic cable, e-mail, and the Internet have made worldwide telecommunication instantaneous.

Perhaps the most striking measure of scientific and technological change can be seen in medicine and public health. At the beginning of the twentieth century, the average American life span was forty-seven years. By the end of the century the average life span was approaching eighty years, thanks to advances in medicine including the development of vaccines and antibiotics, the discovery of powerful diagnostic tools such as X rays, the life-saving technology of cardiac and neonatal care, and improvements in nutrition and the control of infectious disease.

Rapid change is likely to continue throughout the twenty-first century as science reveals more about physical and biological processes such as global warming, viral replication, and electrical conductivity, and as people apply that new knowledge to personal decisions and government policy. Already, for example, an international treaty calls for immediate reductions in industrial and automobile emissions in response to studies that show a potentially dangerous rise in global temperatures is caused by human activity. Taking an active role in determining the direction of future changes depends on education; people must understand the possible uses of scientific research and the effects of the technology that surrounds them.

The Lucent Books Library of Science and Technology profiles key innovations and discoveries that have transformed the modern world. Each title strives to make a complex scientific discovery, technology, or phenomenon understandable and relevant to the reader. Because scientific discovery is rarely straightforward, each title explains the dead ends, fortunate accidents, and basic scientific methods by which the research into the subject proceeded. And every book examines the practical applications of an invention, branch of science, or scientific principle in industry, public health, and personal life, as well as potential future uses and effects based on ongoing research. Fully documented quotations, annotated bibliographies that include both print and electronic sources, glossaries, indexes, and technical illustrations are among the supplemental features designed to point researchers to further exploration of the subject.

Introduction

The Warming of the Earth

In 1958, a scientist named Dr. Charles David Keeling invented an unusual object that caught the attention of the scientific world. The instrument Keeling designed and built was called a manometer, and its purpose was to measure levels of atmospheric carbon dioxide (CO_2). Like all scientists, Keeling knew that CO_2 and other gases existed naturally in the earth's atmosphere. He suspected, though, that CO_2 levels were steadily growing higher. Since the Industrial Revolution, a period of rapid industrial growth in Europe and America during the eighteenth and nineteenth centuries, manufacturing had flourished. This caused more CO_2 than ever before to be pumped into the air. Keeling suspected that this might be lingering in the atmosphere, and some scientists agreed with him. However, until the invention of the manometer there was no way to measure CO_2 levels, so no one had previously been able to prove that levels were higher than normal.

Studies in Hawaii

To get the most objective readings from the manometer, Keeling set up a sampling station on Mauna Loa, a massive volcano two miles above the Pacific Ocean on the island of Hawaii. He believed that this pristine, isolated location would be perfect

9

for his experiment because his measurements would not be influenced by human activities or industrial pollution. After taking a series of readings, Keeling determined that carbon dioxide levels in the atmosphere were 315 parts per million (ppm).

At first, his discovery was not of particular significance because there were no past measurements to use for comparison. In the 1980s, however, Keeling's findings became very significant. Researchers studying ancient ice from Antarctica found that carbon dioxide levels had been about 280 ppm in the 1700s, before the Industrial Revolution had begun. When these measurements were compared with Keeling's findings, the researchers could see that CO_2 had steadily increased over a period of two hundred years. Also during the same period of time, scientists were taking thermometer readings of the earth's sur-

Charles D. Keeling (left) receives the National Medal of Science from President George W. Bush in 2002. Keeling began measuring atmospheric carbon dioxide in 1958.

face, and they showed that the planet's temperature had continued to rise. From that information, scientists determined that a buildup of carbon dioxide was causing the planet to become warmer.

A Hot Topic

When Keeling first began measuring CO_2 on Mauna Loa, the term *global warming* was relatively unknown. With the exception of a few articles scattered throughout scientific publications, there was no publicity about global warming and most people were not aware of it. That is no longer the case, however. Today, global warming has become an environmental issue that makes news headlines nearly every day, and whose significance the National Aeronautic and Space Administration (NASA) describes as follows: "As an Internet search on global warming now attests, the subject has become as rooted in our public consciousness as Madonna or microwave cooking. Perhaps all this attention is deserved. With the possible exception of another world war, a giant asteroid, or an incurable plague, global warming may be the single largest threat to our planet."[1]

In the past hundred years, the earth's surface temperature has risen about one degree Fahrenheit. This may not seem like a significant amount, but scientists want to know what is causing it. In addition, climate measurements show that the most rapid warming in history occurred during the 1990s, with 1998 registering as the hottest year on record. This means that, unlike the past when it took about a thousand years for the earth's temperature to rise by one degree, the current warming is happening at an accelerated rate. Environmental consultant and author Dr. John J. Berger explains why he and many other scientists are alarmed about this rapid rise in the earth's temperature:

> Global temperatures have risen before and nature has adapted. . . . But previous warmings of

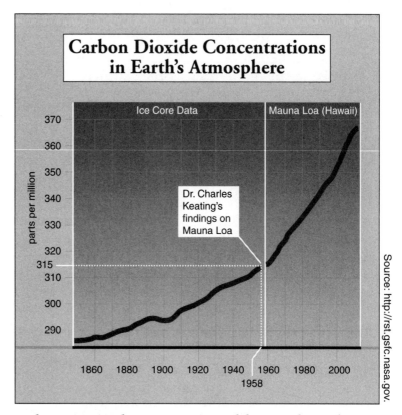

Carbon Dioxide Concentrations in Earth's Atmosphere

Ice Core Data — Mauna Loa (Hawaii)

parts per million

Dr. Charles Keating's findings on Mauna Loa

1860 1880 1900 1920 1940 1960 1980 2000

1958

Source: http://rst.gsfc.nasa.gov.

the magnitude now projected have taken place over millennia, not over decades or centuries. The natural world has had far more time to adapt to the new conditions.[2]

Some scientists insist that this warming trend is due to natural occurrences. Since the earth has existed, its climate has constantly changed, shifting from warm periods to cold periods and then back again. The scientists who are most doubtful about the risks of global warming insist that Earth is a robust planet that has survived fluctuations in temperature over millions of years, and will continue to do so. They believe the current global warming trend is yet another natural cycle that should be expected.

Other scientists, however, strongly disagree. While they acknowledge that the planet has gone through many climate changes in its history, they believe that the current global warming trend is different because it is being caused by humans, not nature.

As with any complex issue, it is impossible to say who is right and who is wrong. No one can predict with certainty whether global warming will continue in the future—and scientists on both sides of the issue are very willing to admit this. Global warming has been a subject of controversy for many years, and there is every reason to believe that the debate will not end anytime soon. If history is any indication, the controversy is likely to become even more heated in the years to come.

Chapter 1

What Is Global Warming?

The mystery of how the earth remains warm enough to sustain life is one that puzzled scientists for hundreds of years. Then during the nineteenth century, a French scientist developed a theory about how the planet was heated, and the mystery was solved. Jean-Baptiste-Joseph Fourier was curious about the sun—specifically, how it was possible that the sun's rays hit the oceans and land and did not just bounce back into space. Fourier knew the earth must somehow have the ability to retain the sun's heat. The very existence of living things was proof of that. So he concluded that only some of the sun's rays escaped back into space, while some were trapped and held by the earth's atmosphere. He compared this function to a giant glass vessel, which let in the sun's light and then trapped and retained its warmth inside.

Fourier wrote about his theory in a paper, published in France in 1824, entitled "General Remarks on the Temperature of the Terrestrial Globe and Planetary Spaces." Six years later he died, and all but a few scientists forgot about his ideas. At that time, no one could have known how important Fourier's theory would become in the future, or that later it would assume the name *greenhouse effect*.

The Earth's Natural Thermostat

What Fourier had discovered was the key to the earth's ability to naturally regulate its own temperature. This is possible because of a natural balance between the sun, the land and oceans, and the atmosphere—a balance that is critical to the survival of all living things.

Earth absorbs only a certain amount of the sun's energy. If it absorbed too much sunlight, the planet would become as hot as the sun and eventually burn up. Actually, about 30 to 40 percent of the sun's heat is absorbed by the land, air, and oceans, while the rest is radiated outward, toward space. As Fourier suspected, though, not all of the sun's energy ends

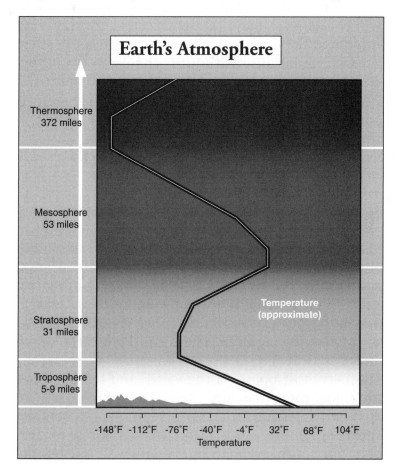

Earth's Atmosphere

Thermosphere
372 miles

Mesosphere
53 miles

Stratosphere
31 miles

Troposphere
5-9 miles

Temperature
(approximate)

-148°F   -112°F   -76°F   -40°F   -4°F   32°F   68°F   104°F
Temperature

up back in space. Some of it remains in the atmos
phere, which is made up of four separate layers: the
troposphere (closest to Earth), the stratosphere, the
mesosphere, and the thermosphere. Surrounding the
earth like a protective blanket, the atmosphere is
made up of invisible gases such as nitrogen, oxygen,
argon, water vapor, ozone, helium, methane, and
carbon dioxide, among others. Gases such as water
vapor, CO_2, methane, and nitrous oxide are composed of molecules that have the ability to trap and
hold heat. So, as the sun's energy is reflected away
from Earth, these heat-trapping gases capture that
energy and then reradiate it toward the surface.

This process is called the greenhouse effect because it is so similar to the way a greenhouse
works—its glass panes allow the sunlight in, while
trapping the heat inside. Thus, the greenhouse effect
is essential because without it the earth would become extremely cold, and it is doubtful that any living thing could survive. The average surface temperature of the planet is now 59 degrees Fahrenheit. If
the atmosphere did not trap and hold heat, the average temperature would be a frigid -0.4 degrees.

Climate vs. Weather

Another term for the earth's average temperature is
global climate. Of course, there are vast differences in
climate throughout the world based on the amount of
sunlight that different regions receive. For instance,
some countries, such as Egypt, Ethiopia, and Iraq, receive intense sunlight all year long, so their climates
are much hotter than climates of countries farther
away from the equator. The South Pole is the opposite. It is located on the continent of Antarctica, at the
southernmost point on the earth, and temperatures
are colder there than anywhere else in the world.

When referring to climate some people actually
mean weather, and while the two are closely related,
they are not the same thing. Weather is more tempo-

rary, fluctuating from month to month, day to day, or even hour to hour. Climate, on the other hand, remains constant. It refers to the average weather and temperatures that are *normal* for a particular region during a month, a season, or a decade. When a permanent weather change occurs, only then is it a statement about climate. Dr. Richard C.J. Somerville, a professor of meteorology at Scripps Institute of Oceanography in California, explains this:

> In a nutshell, the difference between weather and climate is that weather deals with the instantaneous state of the atmosphere. If I say there will be a thunderstorm in London on Thursday afternoon, that's a statement about the weather. But climate deals with longer time scales and with averages and other statistics over space and time. So that if I say London next summer will be drier and warmer than usual, that's a statement about climate. A catchy way to put it is that climate is what you expect, and weather is what you get.[3]

How Climate Has Varied

For as long as the earth has existed, it has experienced changes in climate, including many different periods of warming and cooling. One example of a particularly cold era was the Pleistocene epoch, more commonly called the Ice Age. During the Ice Age, which lasted for thousands of years, approximately 30 percent of the planet's surface was covered with thick ice sheets and enormous rivers of ice known as glaciers. The cold period came to an end around 13,000 B.C., and the earth gradually began to grow warmer.

In the mid-1500s, after centuries of warmth, the earth experienced another extremely cold period called the Little Ice Age. Scientists have discovered records that were kept by people living in Iceland during that time, and those writings have helped

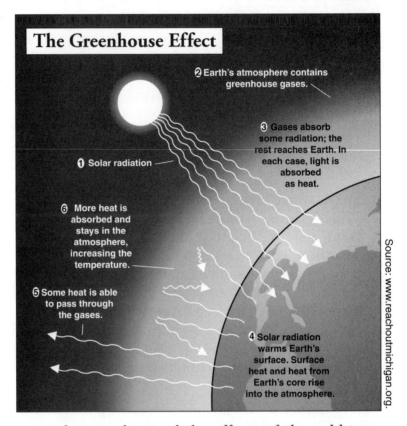

The Greenhouse Effect

❷ Earth's atmosphere contains greenhouse gases.

❸ Gases absorb some radiation; the rest reaches Earth. In each case, light is absorbed as heat.

❶ Solar radiation

❻ More heat is absorbed and stays in the atmosphere, increasing the temperature.

❺ Some heat is able to pass through the gases.

4 Solar radiation warms Earth's surface. Surface heat and heat from Earth's core rise into the atmosphere.

Source: www.reachoutmichigan.org.

researchers understand the effects of the cold temperatures and frozen conditions. For instance, the Icelanders made their living by fishing and they recorded that between 1650 and 1850, their island was completely icebound for several months each year. This caused hardship for them because it hindered their ability to fish. When the temperature began to warm up in 1880, they wrote about their relief that the ice had finally begun to recede, so they could extend their fishing season.

Since the Little Ice Age ended toward the end of the 1800s, the earth has steadily grown warmer. Scientists call this trend global warming, and the National Oceanic and Atmospheric Administration (NOAA) defines it as follows: "The term Global Warming refers to the observation that the atmosphere near the Earth's surface is warming, without any implications for the cause or magnitude. This warming is one of many kinds of climate change that the Earth has gone through in the past and will continue to go through in the future."[4] Because the planet has experienced such periods of warming and cooling throughout its history, some scientists believe that the current warming is just one more product of nature—that the earth is simply doing what it has always done in the past.

Continental Drift

Since the earth has existed, many natural phenomena have affected its changes in climate. One example is continental drift, which is a theory accepted by most scientists and historians. It is based on the belief that 200 million years ago the earth was one large landmass, or supercontinent, called Pangaea. Over millions of years, Pangaea split into separate chunks of land, forming the continents that currently exist. Scientists studying the continents discovered that their coastlines are shaped as though they once fit together, similar to the pieces of a jigsaw

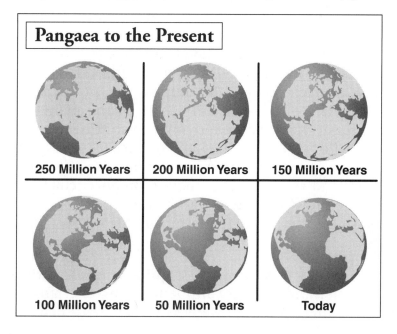

Pangaea to the Present

| 250 Million Years | 200 Million Years | 150 Million Years |
| 100 Million Years | 50 Million Years | Today |

puzzle. Scientists have also found identical plant and animal fossils, as well as rocks and sediments, on the coastlines of both South America and Africa. This is further proof that in ancient times these two continents were joined as one.

The formation of separate continents caused some areas of the earth to move to new locations over millions of years. Scientists believe this resulted in extreme climatic changes. Whereas Antarctica is now a frozen continent, studies of plant fossils confirm that it was once a tropical place, near the equator, where lush, swampy vegetation thrived. At the other extreme, evidence of glaciers has been found in the southern part of the African continent. This is likely to mean that Africa, now one of the world's hottest regions, was once very cold—possibly even as cold as the South Pole is today.

Although the most dramatic phase of continental drift happened millions of years ago, the continents are still on the move. This is explained by plate tectonics, which theorizes that the earth's crust is divided into twelve gigantic chunks (or plates) that are constantly shifting. Beneath them is the earth's constantly churning core of molten rock, known as the mantle. The plates float on top of the mantle, continuously sliding around, crunching against each other, and pulling apart. In the same way that continental drift changed the planet in the past, the constant moving and shifting of plate tectonics continues to shape the oceans and land. As a result, mountains form and oceans shift direction, and there are also changes in air circulation, or the ongoing motion of the atmosphere over the earth. As these changes occur, climate is affected.

Ocean Activity

The earth's oceans play a major role in regulating climate, and strongly influence climate changes. These huge bodies of water cover about 70 percent of the planet's surface, and they have a tremendous capacity to hold and store heat from the sun. Most heat that escapes from oceans is in the form of water vapor, which is the most plentiful atmospheric gas. When ocean waters become warmer than usual, such as when they absorb higher-than-average levels of sunlight, they emit more water vapor into the atmosphere. This affects the earth's climate in two ways: Because water vapor is a powerful heat-trapping gas, more water vapor means that more heat is retained in the atmosphere; and water vapor contributes to the formation of clouds, which shade the earth and have an overall cooling effect.

Ocean currents also exert a strong influence on the earth's climate. Like great rivers, these masses of water are constantly on the move—twisting, turning, and winding their way through the oceans. As they move along regular paths, currents carry the oceans' stored heat across the planet. One example of a major ocean current is the Gulf Stream, which carries warm water from the Caribbean Sea up the east coast of the United States, and across the North Atlantic to the west coasts of Great Britain and northern Europe. Because of the Gulf Stream, these areas are much warmer than they would be if it did not exist. Other ocean currents function in much the same way.

When currents slow down or change direction, the earth's climate is affected. Dr. Robert B. Gagosian, president of the Woods Hole Oceanographic Institution, explains how the oceans influence worldwide climates:

> The ocean isn't a stagnant bathtub. It circulates heat around the planet like the heating and cooling system in your house. The atmosphere and oceans are equal partners in creating Earth's climate. The atmosphere is a rabbit. It moves fast. Rapid changes in atmospheric circulation

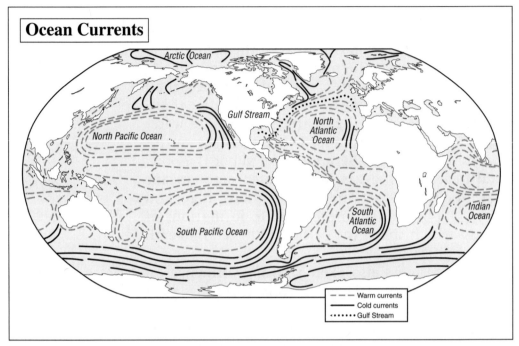

Ocean Currents

cause storms, cold spells, or heat waves that play out over several days. The ocean, on the other hand, is a turtle. It may take years or decades or even millennia for similar "disturbances" to circulate through the ocean. But the ocean is a big turtle. It stores about 1,000 times more heat than the atmosphere. So changes in ocean circulation can set the stage for large-scale long-term climate changes.[5]

Volcanoes

Among the powerful natural forces that can influence the earth's climate are volcanoes. When volcanoes erupt, they send huge clouds of volcanic material—including sulfur dioxide, water vapor, dust, and ash—many miles into the atmosphere. The volcanic material forms a thick haze that prevents sunlight from reaching Earth and can cause global cooling. This is especially true during the most violent eruptions, such as one that occurred over seventy thousand years ago on the island of Sumatra. A volcano known as Toba erupted with such immense force that it released more than six hundred cubic miles of sulfur and ash into the sky. According to geologist William Hutton, the eruption, which buried most of India under ash, caused significant changes in the global climate. He describes the effects of Toba: "This was a true cataclysm . . . because it had significant worldwide effects. An estimated 75 percent of the Northern Hemisphere's plants may have died. At the end of the first six years of climate cooling, a thousand-year ice age began. Perhaps only a few thousand people, living

Volcanic ash billows skyward during the 1991 eruption of Mount Pinatubo in the Philippines. Volcanic eruptions can dramatically affect global climate.

in isolated pockets in Africa, Europe, and Asia survived."[6]

A more recent example of volcanic activity occurred
at Mount Pinatubo, which erupted in the Philippines
in 1991. The eruption was Mount Pinatubo's first in
over four hundred years, and it was considered the
most violent volcanic event of the twentieth century. During a series of eruptions that lasted for
seven days, clouds of volcanic material were blasted
twelve miles high, and remnants of the sulfur and
ash reached as far away as Russia and North America.
Afterward, scientists estimated that the eruption had
caused a decrease in global temperatures of about one
degree Fahrenheit that lasted for about two years.

The Earth's Orbit and Tilt

The tilt of the planet is another natural phenomenon that can affect climate. As Earth travels around
the sun, a process that takes 365 days, it is not point-
ing straight up and down. Instead, it is tilted at a
23.45-degree angle. The greater the tilt, the more
sunshine the North Pole and South Pole receive during the summer. So, if the earth's tilt were to change,
the climate would change as well. For example, with
the earth's current tilt, it remains cold enough at the
poles to keep much of their surfaces permanently
covered with ice. If the planet's tilt were to increase,
the poles would receive more sun in the summer,
and the ice cover would likely begin to shrink. If,
however, the earth's tilt were to decrease, the poles
would be colder and the ice sheets and glaciers
would probably expand.

Earth is not perfectly still during its orbital process.
It actually wobbles in space, and that can cause the
degree of the tilt to change. This wobbling also
causes variations in the planet's distance from the
sun, which affects the amount of solar energy that
reaches the surface. One profound example of how
changes in Earth's orbit and tilt affect climate is the

Sahara Desert in northern Africa. By using a computer simulation of the earth's climate, German researchers discovered that until about four thousand years ago, the Sahara was a fertile area where agriculture thrived and people could farm the land. Over a period of hundreds of years, Earth's tilt changed, causing the African continent to tilt closer to the sun. As a result, temperature rose dramatically and the vast desert that exists today was created. Scientists speculate that when the agricultural land evolved into desert, it may have forced early civilizations to leave the area and settle along the valleys of the Nile, the Tigris, and the Euphrates Rivers.

Clouds

Areas like the Sahara Desert have the hottest climates on the earth because they are close to the equator, and also because they have very little cloud cover. Clouds are formed when water vapor in the air rises into the sky, and then cools down and condenses. This happens most often in areas where there is an abundance of water. Because deserts have virtually no water, there is almost no moisture in the air. So, clouds rarely form in these areas and there is almost no precipitation. In other regions of the world where more clouds hover overhead, regular rainfall and snow are common and temperatures are cooler.

Clouds are a powerful influence on global climate because they block much of the sun's energy, reflecting it back into space before it can be absorbed by Earth or the atmosphere. So, the thicker and more plentiful clouds are, the cooler the earth will be. If there were no clouds in the sky, the planet would be about twenty degrees hotter than it is today.

Continued Study

Scientists are in agreement that climate can be influenced by natural causes. Regardless of where they stand on the global warming issue, all believe that it

North Africa's Sahara Desert was once fertile land before a change in the tilt of the earth's axis caused the temperature in the area to rise dramatically.

is important to continue studying the earth's climate, including climatic changes throughout history. Only through this research can they learn whether these changes are a product of nature or the result of human activities—or perhaps even both.

Dr. Wallace S. Broecker, a geology professor at Columbia University in New York City, and a well-known scientific researcher, offers his perspective on the importance of climate research:

> As I sometimes tell my students, the folks in the back room who designed our planet were pretty clever. We have clear evidence that different parts of the earth's climate system are linked in very subtle yet dramatic ways. The climate system has jumped from one mode of operation to another in the past. We are trying to understand how the earth's climate system is engineered, so we can understand what it takes to trigger mode switches. Until we do, we cannot make good predictions about future climate change.[7]

Chapter 2

The Study of Climate Change

Scientists learn about climate and how it has changed by studying climates of the past. By analyzing changes that have occurred in the earth's temperature over time, scientists can gain a better understanding of global warming, and make determinations about its possible causes.

Scientists have discovered ways to study the earth's climate, going back as far as thousands, or even millions, of years. Those who specialize in studying ancient climates are known as paleoclimatologists, a name derived from the Greek root word *paleo*, which means ancient. Paleoclimatologists use natural elements in the environment to find "proxy climate data" related to the past. When they study these types of data, these scientists typically use several different methods, so they are assured of forming the most accurate analysis possible.

Tree Rings Tell a Story

One way that paleoclimatologists unlock the secrets of ancient climates is by studying the rings in certain types of trees, such as the redwoods and giant sequoias found in California and different varieties of pines. As a tree grows, it adds a new layer of wood to its trunk every year. This forms a ring, and the age of the tree can be determined by counting the number of these annual growth rings.

Many trees live to be hundreds of years old, and some live for thousands of years. The oldest trees on Earth are the bristlecone pines, many of which are found in the Ancient Bristlecone Pine Forest in California's White Mountains. The average age of these trees is 1,000 years, and a few are more than 4,000 years old. In 1964, before there were environmental laws to protect ancient trees, a particular bristlecone pine named Prometheus was cut down. After analyzing the tree's rings, scientists determined that the tree had been 4,862 years old—the oldest living thing on Earth.

Paleoclimatologists can learn more than just the age of a tree by studying its rings. They can determine what sort of climate conditions existed during its life by analyzing the thickness of each tree ring. Thick rings are a sign of favorable climate, abundant rainfall, and good growing conditions. Thin rings indicate poor growing conditions and lack of rain, as well as natural disasters such as droughts, floods, and volcanoes.

Samples from trees can be obtained in several different ways. Scientists do not want to needlessly destroy living trees, so they cut cross sections only from dead trees, logs, or stumps. These can be found intact on the ground, buried deep in the ground, or submerged in water. Tree remnants that have been buried for hundreds or even thousands of years have been found and analyzed. For samples from living trees, scientists use a tool known as an increment borer to drill a thin hole into the trunk. Then, a core sample of wood about the size of a drinking straw is extracted for analysis. This boring does not cause damage to the tree because when the sample has been removed, the tree naturally closes the small opening just as it would close a wound caused by insects or weather.

Once the wood samples are obtained, scientists return to the laboratory to measure and date them. Cross sections of dead trees are often old and brittle; and scientists may need to glue pieces together—or mount them on a hard wooden surface—for added protection. Cores that are taken from living trees are soft, so they must be dried before being mounted for examination. The next step is to sand the samples or trim them with razor blades to produce a smooth surface that makes the fine details of the rings more visible. Then scientists can examine the samples under a microscope and record their findings about the tree's history.

Tree rings like these not only tell scientists the age of the tree, but they also provide a record of climate change over the centuries.

Clues Beneath the Water

Another way paleoclimatologists analyze historical climates is by studying samples of varves—layers of silt and clay that are deposited year after year on the bottoms of glacial lakes and ponds. Varves provide natural climate records going back several thousand years. They consist of two layers: a thick, light-colored layer of silt and fine sand that forms in the spring and summer, and a thinner, dark-colored layer of clay that forms in the fall and winter and sinks to the bottom.

Varve thickness varies from year to year, usually according to the climate and the amount of rain that falls during a particular season. For example, when temperatures are especially hot and dry and there is little rain, less soil is washed into the water, and the varve layers are thinner. On the other hand, when spring and summer rains are heavy, a greater amount of soil is washed into lakes and ponds, and this causes thicker varves. Paleoclimatologists collect varve samples by using long, hollow tubes to drill into the soft bottoms of lakes and ponds. Once they extract this material, they analyze the different layers that have been deposited over time.

Clues about ancient climates are not found only in bodies of freshwater such as lakes and ponds, but are also buried in sediment that has settled in the earth's deep oceans. Robert B. Gagosian says that by studying these sediments, called deep-sea cores, scientists can reconstruct the history of ocean climates spanning thousands of years. He describes this research, and explains why it is so important:

> Preserved in the sediments are the fossil remains of microscopic organisms that settle to the seafloor. They accumulate over time in layers . . . that delineate many important aspects of past climate. For instance, certain organisms are found only in colder, polar waters and never live in warmer waters. They can reveal where and when cold surface waters existed—and didn't exist—in the past. From records like these, we know that about 12,800 years ago, North Atlantic waters cooled dramatically—and so did the North Atlantic region. This large cooling in Earth's climate . . . lasted for about 1,300 years. This period is called the Younger Dryas, and it is just one of several periods when Earth's climate changed very rapidly from warm to cold conditions, and then back to warm again.[8]

To gather data from oceans, scientists spend two to three months on research cruises. Using highly specialized equipment, they remove samples of deep-sea cores from beneath the surface of the ocean floor. These long cylinders of sediment provide valuable evidence about changes in ocean temperatures that were caused by fluctuations in climate.

Scientists also gather and study sediment from different bodies of water to gather pollen. This powdery substance, produced by flowering plants each growing season, is carried in the wind, and billions of grains of it end up buried at the bottoms of lakes, ponds, rivers, and oceans. The oldest pollen becomes fossilized, and is often found in sedimentary rocks that have formed over thousands of years. Since all plant species produce their own unique type of pollen, scientists can

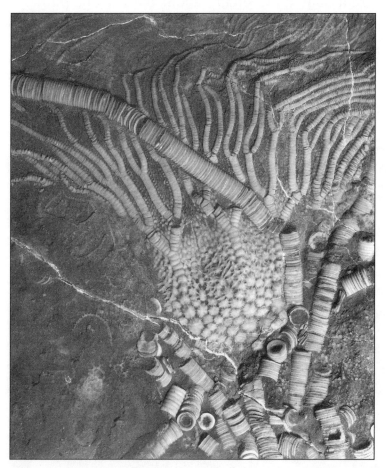

Marine fossils such as these provide clues about climatic conditions during the fossilized creatures' lifetime.

tell what plants grew during certain periods in the earth's history. Also, they can make accurate estimates about changes in climate. This is because for every type of pollen, certain habitat conditions would have been necessary for that particular kind of plant to survive and thrive.

Underwater Cities

Coral reefs can also provide important clues to climates of the past. There are many different types of corals, but "stony corals" build huge reefs in warm, tropical seas. Coral reefs are made up of millions of tiny animals called coral polyps, which are cousins of the jellyfish. Although polyps differ in size, they are usually quite small—about the size of a pinhead. The polyps form protective skeletons by extracting calcium carbonate—the same material that is found in teeth, bones, and shells—from the salty, tropical ocean waters in which they live. As the skeletons grow, coral reefs are formed, and become as hard as rocks. These huge structures are often called under-

Coral reefs have grown to gigantic proportions over the centuries. Scientists study a reef's layers to learn about long-term climate changes.

water cities because they are the largest biologically built structures on Earth.

Every time a piece of coral skeleton is created, it leaves a record of the conditions under which it was created. For instance, when water temperatures change, the chemistry (or makeup) of the skeletons also changes. The result is that coral formed in the summer looks different than coral formed in the winter, so it is easy for paleoclimatologists to know in which season the coral was formed. As coral reefs grow, growth bands form that are very much like the growth rings found in trees. Sometimes these bands are visible to the naked eye, and sometimes scientists can only see the bands by x-raying them.

To gather samples of coral, scientists go on diving expeditions in tropical areas, where they search for massive coral reefs built by stony coral. Using drills that are connected to a compressor mechanism on a ship, the divers extract cores of the coral, much the same way cores are extracted from trees. Their goal is to drill in areas where the most growth has occurred, as the NOAA explains: "Think of the coral's structure as being very similar to an onion sliced in half, with a new ring added each year. If you wanted to drill into an onion to sample as many rings as possible, you would core from the surface directly towards the center. This is exactly how scientists go about getting as long a sample as possible from each coral."[9]

Once scientists have carefully extracted the cores, they label and box them for shipment to their laboratories. There they x-ray the coral to examine the growth bands, which helps them determine the seasons in which the corals grew. With this proxy climate data, paleoclimatologists can analyze how climates fluctuated in the reef over hundreds of years.

Unlocking Secrets in Ancient Ice

Just as scientists gain clues about climate from warm, tropical seas, they can also gather knowledge from the coldest places on the earth. In fact, some of the most revealing indicators of historical climates come from studies of glaciers and ice sheets in the world's polar regions. To gather samples of ancient ice, scientists travel to remote areas of Antarctica, where temperatures can dip as low as -129 degrees Fahrenheit.

Massive ice domes, ice sheets, and glaciers are found in the Arctic and in Antarctica. These ice formations developed over hundreds of thousands of years as layers of snow pressed together. More precipitation continued to pile on top of the snow, squeezing the layers and slowly forming ice. As the layers accumulated, air bubbles were trapped inside, forming distinct lines that can be counted as easily as tree rings. Scientists examine the layers to determine the age of the ice and the approximate climate during a given period. They can also tell how much snow fell during a year, as well as what kind of air, dust, volcanic material, and other microscopic particles—including pollution—existed at the time the ice sheets were formed.

About 98 percent of the world's ancient ice is located in the polar regions, and most scientists choose to focus on those areas when they study ice. Others, however, believe that ice from tropical areas is even more crucial in order to understand how climates have changed over time. Lonnie Thompson is a glaciologist who studies ancient ice in areas such as South America and Africa. These regions have hot, tropical climates, but they also have very high mountain ranges where ice sheets and glaciers can be found. Thompson sometimes climbs mountains three or four miles high. On one expedition, he and his team worked for three weeks at an altitude above twenty-three thousand feet.

Thompson's work is challenging as well as dangerous. With the help of local porters and animals called yaks, he and his team haul about six tons of

equipment to the top of a mountain. There they must endure bone-chilling cold, the threat of avalanches, and such high altitudes that it is hard to breathe. There is also the risk of frequent windstorms. One particularly fierce storm knocked Thompson's tent from its moorings and nearly blew him off a mountain.

During a typical expedition, Thompson and his team accumulate about four tons of ice samples, which means they must drag ten tons of equipment back down the mountain. He says it is well worth the effort, though, and he explains why he thinks ice is the best possible archive of the history of the earth's climate: "Understanding how the climate system works and has worked in the natural system is absolutely essential for any prediction of what's going to happen to the climate in the future."[10] Thompson adds that by examining ancient ice, scientists can

This mammoth Antarctic glacier dwarfs the scientist at its base. Glacial ice cores give scientists a historical record of climate changes.

determine climate conditions and changes over thousands of years in the past.

Whether they explore ice domes in Antarctica, glaciers in Tibet, or ice sheets at the top of Africa's Kilimanjaro, scientists gather samples by using powerful drills to bore into the ice. The deeper the drill goes—and that can be several miles—the further it travels back in time. (Thompson's oldest ice sample is more than seven hundred thousand years old.) After drilling, scientists extract cores of ice and carefully package them in insulated containers, so the samples can be sent to their laboratories for analysis. Thompson says that by collecting ice samples, scientists can compile a frozen history of the earth.

Modern Instruments for Measuring

The reason scientists use proxy climate data obtained from ice, trees, coral reefs, and other products of nature is because they want to understand what the earth's climate was like long ago. Scientists use these types of data along with modern devices so they can learn more about how climate has changed over time, as well as how historical and current climates compare with each other.

Thermometers, which measure temperatures of the earth's surface, have been used to determine climate for only about 130 years. Some scientists, like Dr. S. Fred Singer, who is an atmospheric physicist, question the accuracy of thermometers because they are often used near cities, which are warmer than open country. Singer explains his views: "You have to be very careful with surface record. . . . As cities expand, they get warmer. And therefore they affect the readings. And it's very difficult to eliminate this—what's called the urban heat island effect."[11]

Dr. John Firor, a senior scientist at the National Center for Atmospheric Research, says it is true that cities are generally warmer than open country. He adds, however, that thermometers can provide accurate measurements even in cities, and he explains how:

> One can find empty holes in the ground—abandoned oil wells, for instance—and put down a long line of thermometers. This allows measurement of the temperature of soil or rocks many levels down. The reason this works is because over time, the warmth at the surface is conducted to deeper levels. So, the temperature deep down in the hole relates to the surface temperature of long ago. This is also true when the surface is cold—the coolness is conducted down over time. Many holes have been measured in recent years, and what we've found is that the record of past temperatures confirms what is measured from carefully placed surface thermometers.[12]

Watching from Space

A highly sophisticated way of monitoring the earth's climate is through the use of satellites. Since the 1950s, NASA satellites have been observing Earth's atmosphere, oceans, land, snow, and ice from high in space. The data they provide can help scientists develop a better understanding of how these different elements interact with each other to influence climate and weather.

One example is *Terra*, a satellite that was launched by NASA in 1999. *Terra*, named after the Latin word for land, is about the size of a small school bus, and its mission is to circle Earth for about six years. The satellite is fitted with a variety of sensitive instruments that are designed for specific purposes, such as measuring the chemical composition of clouds and gauging the temperature of the land. *Terra*'s MICR instrument has nine separate digital cameras that take pictures of Earth from different angles, while its MOPITT instrument uses light sensors to measure concentrations of methane gas and carbon monoxide, two heat-trapping gases. The satellite's instrument MODIS measures cloud cover and also monitors changes in Earth due to fires, earthquakes, droughts, or flooding. An instrument called CERES measures both incoming energy from the sun and reflected energy from Earth and studies the role that clouds play in this energy balance.

In the spring of 2002, NASA launched another satellite called *Aqua*, whose mission is to gather information about the earth's bodies of water. *Aqua* will circle the planet every sixteen days for six years, and its sophisticated instruments will measure such things as global precipitation, evaporation, humidity, and ocean circulation. This data will help scientists better understand the balance between the earth's oceans, land, and atmosphere, as well as how

The Aqua *satellite gathers data about a hurricane visible on Earth's surface.* Aqua's *data helps scientists understand global climatic changes.*

global climate change influences this balance.

In the future, NASA will launch more satellites to study global climate change. The organization describes the goal for these studies as follows:

> As we learn more about our home planet, new questions arise, drawing us deeper into the complexities of Earth's climate system. We don't know the answers to many other important questions, like: Is the current warming trend temporary, or just the beginning of an accelerating increase in global temperatures? As temperatures rise, how will this affect weather patterns, food production systems, and sea level? Are the number and size of clouds increasing and, if so, how will this affect the amount of incoming and reflected sunlight, as well as the heat emitted from Earth's surface? . . . How will climate change affect human health, natural resources, and human economies in the future? NASA's Earth Observing System, and Terra in particular, will help scientists answer these questions, as well as some we don't even know to ask yet.[13]

Unraveling the Mystery

Scientists are the first to say that there are many unknown factors involved in the study of global climate change. Products of nature such as ice cores, coral reefs, ocean and lake sediments, and trees can offer valuable clues about changing climates in the ancient past. Modern instruments like satellites can provide knowledge about current activities affecting the earth's land, oceans, and atmosphere. Assembling the pieces of this global environmental puzzle is the focus of scientists and researchers all over the world. They know for sure that the earth is warming—and using the many tools available to them, it is their mission to find out why.

Chapter 3

The Human Contribution

Scientists know that the earth is warming and most of them acknowledge that it has warmed about one degree in the past hundred years. What many of them find alarming is how quickly that change has occurred. Throughout the planet's history there have been periods of warming and cooling, but the average rate of change has been about one degree per thousand years—so the current global warming appears to be happening ten times faster than ever before. Many scientists believe that this is the result of anthropogenic actions, which are caused by human beings rather than nature. Dr. Stephen H. Schneider, biological sciences professor at Stanford University, is one scientist who believes that people are to blame for the current global warming, as he explains:

> Humans are not simply passengers holding a temporary ticket on planet Earth's ride through the galaxy. We are actively altering the surface of the land and the composition of the atmosphere. These factors affect the natural flows of energy and materials around the planet and in turn are altering the climate. And while it usually takes nature thousands of years to create several degrees of temperature change on a glob-

ally sustained basis, human beings can do so in a century or less.[14]

Fossil Fuels: Friend or Foe?

Schneider and other like-minded scientists insist that this accelerated warming is caused by greenhouse gases that humans are adding to the atmosphere. That is why scientists often use the term *greenhouse warming* to describe the current warming of the earth. Richard Somerville shares his views on the cause of this increase in temperature: "The concern is that we human beings are modifying that greenhouse effect by adding to the atmosphere gases that increase the natural abundance of these so-called gases. . . . We're adding them through lots of processes, the most important single one of which is burning fossil fuel (coal and oil and natural gas), which releases carbon dioxide."[15]

Fossil fuels were formed hundreds of millions of years ago from the fossilized remains of plants and animals. After the organisms died and decomposed,

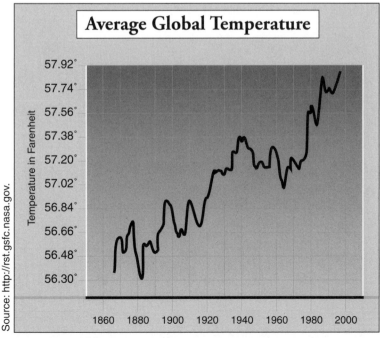

Source: http://rst.gsfc.nasa.gov.

they were eventually buried under hundreds or thousands of feet of mud, rock, and sand. Over time, pressure and heat from the earth compacted the material into layers of sedimentary rock. Different types of fossil fuels were formed based on the types of animals and plants that had decomposed, how long this material was buried, and the degree of temperature and pressure that existed.

Coal is a fossil fuel that has been used since about 1000 B.C., but during the Industrial Revolution its use began to soar. Since coal was found to be both plentiful and cheap, it was burned to power the rapidly growing industry throughout Europe and America. Historian Gale Christianson describes the pollution of this period: "By the mid-1800s, the tall chimneys [of factories], each constructed of a million or more bricks and hundreds of tons of mortar, had far eclipsed the great cathedrals of medieval Europe, rising as high as 450 feet. They spewed their burden of gases and effluents high into the atmosphere round the clock, where it was believed the pollutants would disperse without harm."[16]

During the Industrial Revolution, coal-burning factories like the one in this drawing contributed a significant amount of carbon dioxide to Earth's atmosphere.

For many years, coal was considered the primary fuel. It was used not only for manufacturing, but also for everything from heating homes to providing power for railroad trains and steamships. Today, coal is used by industry to manufacture such products as steel and cement, but its leading use is in making electricity. Power plants use coal to heat water to high temperatures until it turns into steam, which then rotates large turbines to create electricity. In the United States, more than 50 percent of all electrical plants use coal, which also provides power for about 40 percent of the total electricity generated throughout the world.

The other two fossil fuels, oil and natural gas, are also used to produce electricity, but not as often as coal. Oil and gas are primarily used to heat homes and factories, as well as fuel all forms of transportation from buses to ships and motorcycles to airplanes.

All fossil fuels release carbon whenever they are burned, but coal has a much higher carbon content than either oil or gas. The Union of Concerned Scientists says that coal is a main contributor toward global warming because so much electricity is produced from coal-burning power plants. The group also says that these power plants are the single largest source of atmospheric CO_2. Each year, about 7 billion tons of carbon are released through the burning of fossil fuels; and when this reacts with oxygen, carbon dioxide is created—more than 20 billion tons of it.

The Planet's Natural Balance

Carbon dioxide is a colorless, odorless gas that is naturally present in the atmosphere, but only in tiny amounts. In fact, oxygen and nitrogen comprise about 99 percent of atmospheric gases, while all the other gases—including CO_2—total just 1 percent. Yet even though carbon dioxide is only a trace gas, it is essential for life. Its powerful heat-trapping capabilities help keep the earth warm, and CO_2 is also necessary in order for all types of plants to live and grow. That is because of its role in photosynthesis, the process by which plants combine light energy from the sun with CO_2 and water to produce their own food.

Carbon dioxide is created naturally when all living things breathe. For example, the bodies of humans and animals contain about 18 percent carbon. Each time they inhale they take in oxygen, which mixes with the carbon in their bodies and is then exhaled as carbon dioxide in a process known as respiration. CO_2 is also formed naturally when living things die and decompose. The carbon that has been stored in the body of the plant, animal, or human is released into the soil over time. Eventually it reacts with oxygen in the soil and releases carbon dioxide into the air.

Together, all these processes make up a natural system that keeps carbon dioxide levels in balance. As long as the amount of CO_2 that is added to the air through respiration and decay is the same as the amount that is taken out, that balance is maintained. However, over the past hundred years, atmospheric concentrations of carbon dioxide have increased by about one-third—and in that same period of time the earth has warmed by about one degree Fahrenheit. Many scientists believe this is not a coincidence.

According to John J. Berger, carbon dioxide is more responsible for changing the earth's climate than any other gas, as he explains:

> This is because we add more of it to the atmosphere—by far—than any other. Amazing as it may seem, by adding only a few hundredths of a percent of it to the air, we change our climate. The Earth's temperature and the concentration of carbon dioxide in the atmosphere have risen and fallen together for at least the past 420,000

years—as far back in time as our instruments can probe. . . . Only in the past 150 years, however, have human actions actually begun markedly raising the carbon dioxide levels in the atmosphere.[17]

Berger says that more than 65 percent of the warming that has occurred over the past century has been caused by the carbon dioxide added to the atmosphere by humans.

The First Warning

The first scientist to propose that increased carbon dioxide could alter the atmosphere was a Swedish chemist named Svante Arrhenius. In the late 1890s, he studied the paper that had been written by Jean-Baptiste-Joseph Fourier about seventy years before. Arrhenius agreed with Fourier about the role of heat-trapping gases in the atmosphere, and he was intrigued with the scientist's theory that the earth acted like a giant glass vessel that trapped and held heat. Arrhenius took the theory one step further, though. He suspected that humans were causing the gases to accumulate at a faster-than-normal rate because of the burning of fossil fuels such as coal. Arrhenius thought it was logical that as more fossil fuels were burned, more carbon was released into the atmosphere. He believed this could cause atmospheric carbon dioxide levels to rise significantly— which, he reasoned, would trap more of the sun's energy and make the earth hotter. For this reason, he used the example of a hothouse, or greenhouse, model to describe the warming of the planet.

In 1895, Arrhenius presented a paper to a prominent scientific group in Stockholm, Sweden. The paper was called "On the Influence of Carbonic Acid in the Air upon the Temperature of the Ground," and it expressed his belief that higher levels of carbon dioxide in the atmosphere could raise the earth's

Swedish chemist Svante Arrhenius believed that carbon dioxide would accumulate in the atmosphere and cause global warming.

temperature. Arrhenius was not alarmed by the potential for global warming; in fact, he thought that it might be a good thing for the planet. And even though he predicted that atmospheric concentrations of CO_2 would double, he believed that it would be several thousand years before this happened.

Revealing Discoveries

During the following years, some scientists explored Arrhenius's theories about the relationship between carbon dioxide and climate. However, most scientists paid no attention. There was no way to prove that CO_2 was building up in the atmosphere because there were no instruments to measure it; and it was assumed the earth's oceans would prevent carbon dioxide from accumulating in the atmosphere because they could absorb gas. Then in the 1950s, Roger Revelle and Hans Suess, both scientists from Scripps Institute of Oceanography, published a research paper challenging that belief. They concluded that there were limits to how much CO_2 the oceans could absorb, and that the excess carbon dioxide produced by industry and automobiles would remain in the air and eventually warm the planet. Still, the majority of scientists found this theory hard to believe. These beliefs did not begin to change until Charles David Keeling designed and built his manometer. His ability to measure carbon dioxide levels piqued the interest of other scientists.

The real turning point came during the 1980s. Researchers at the Polar Plateau in Vostok, East Antarctica, drilled thousands of miles into a glacier and extracted an ice core that dated back more than one hundred thousand years. By analyzing air bubbles trapped in the ice, the scientists were able to confirm that carbon dioxide levels had risen steadily since the mid-1700s. At that point, more scientists began to pay attention.

Over the following years, measurements continued to be taken at the Mauna Loa Observatory, and carbon dioxide levels showed steady increases each year. By the year 2000, atmospheric concentrations of carbon dioxide had risen to more than 368 ppm—a 17 percent jump from the 1950s when the first measurements were taken. These findings meant that not only were CO_2 levels rising, they were rising fast.

Even scientists who doubt that global warming is a problem admit that humans have increased the amount of CO_2 in the atmosphere. For instance, Dr. Patrick J. Michaels says that predictions about global warming have been proven inaccurate because the earth has warmed at a much slower rate than some scientists said it would. For this reason, he believes that the global warming issue has been blown out of proportion. However, he also acknowledges that CO_2 levels have risen and that humans have played at least some role in the increase, as he explains:

> It has been known since 1872 that water vapor and carbon dioxide are the principal "greenhouse"

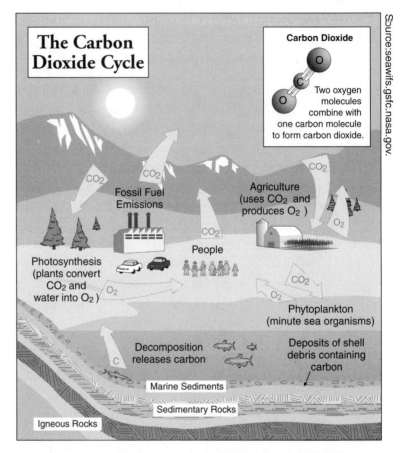

gases in the atmosphere, and that increasing their concentration should elevate the temperature in the lower atmosphere. What has been a subject of contention ever since, is the amount and character of the warming. Because of all of the atmospheric greenhouse gases emitted by human activity, we have progressed to roughly a 60% increase in the equivalent natural carbon dioxide greenhouse effect.[18]

Deforestation

Burning fossil fuels is not the only human activity that releases carbon dioxide into the air. The destruction of the world's forests creates about 30 percent of all anthropogenic greenhouse gases. Living trees breathe in carbon and breathe out oxygen, and when they are cut down, huge concentrations of CO_2 are released into the air. When trees are burned, the effects are doubly harmful to the environment.

In many parts of the world, especially in tropical countries such as Brazil, Indonesia, Burma, and Thailand, rain forests are considered more of a problem than an asset. In order to clear land for planting crops or raising livestock, the forests are chopped down and burned, a practice called slash-and-burn agriculture. The environmental group Rainforest Action Network says that only about half of the world's forests that existed a thousand years ago remain today. NASA predicts what will happen if the destruction of forests is not stopped: "The loss of tropical rain forest is more profound than merely destruction of beautiful areas. If the current rate of deforestation continues, the world's rain forests will vanish within 100 years—causing unknown effects on global climate and eliminating the majority of plant and animal species on the planet."[19]

Cutting down and burning forests releases carbon dioxide and other heat-trapping gases into the atmosphere. That is not the only damage that is done, however. The immense green canopies of the world's

This denuded landscape was once lush tropical forest. Deforestation causes atmospheric carbon dioxide to build up rapidly.

forests absorb and store enormous amounts of carbon dioxide through the process of photosynthesis—so much so that scientists refer to them as "carbon sinks." By destroying the forests people also ruin the earth's natural ability to keep the environment in balance.

Beyond CO_2—the Perils of Methane

Carbon dioxide accounts for most of the anthropogenic gases in the atmosphere, but other heat-trapping gases have been building up over time. Methane comprises about 20 percent of these, and concentrations of it are increasing at the rate of about 1 percent each year. Also, while methane is not as plentiful as CO_2, it is about thirty times more powerful at absorbing heat in the atmosphere—which means its potential for contributing to global warming is greater than any other gas.

Methane is released in a number of ways. It is emitted into the atmosphere during the burning of fossil fuels, and also when forests are burned. It escapes from the ground during oil drilling and coal mining, and is often vented into the air to prevent underground mine explosions. Natural gas is about 90 percent methane, and when natural gas is extracted from the ground, methane can escape through cracked or leaking pipelines. Methane is also formed during the decay of garbage. In the United States alone, about 10 million tons of food waste is disposed of each year by commercial restaurants and households. When organic materials such as food scraps, grass and tree clippings, leaves, and wood debris are hauled to landfills, they are buried. Unlike carbon dioxide, methane forms without oxygen; so as the materials decompose beneath the ground, methane is eventually released into the atmosphere.

Many people are surprised to learn that a major contributor to methane gas is the raising of livestock. When animals such as cattle, sheep, goats, horses, pigs, and camels eat grass and hay, the food is broken down in their digestive systems by bacteria. Methane is expelled into the air when these animals belch, and when their manure decomposes. In countries where there is a high amount of agriculture, farm animals are often the largest source of methane. In Scotland, for instance, farm animals produce more than 45 percent of the country's total methane, while in New Zealand the number is much higher: nearly 90 percent. Currently, the worldwide cattle population is increasing faster than the human population, and as more cattle are raised, more methane gas is created.

Rice agriculture is another leading source of global methane emissions, and it is responsible for about 10 percent of the anthropogenic methane in the atmosphere. Rice is the staple food for more than half of the world's people, especially in Asian countries such as China and India. As the population of these countries continues to grow, more rice must be produced. For much of the growing season, rice farmers flood their rice paddies with water to help control bugs and weeds. Mud-dwelling bacteria and other organisms break down organic material in the water-logged soil to produce methane. Then, as the hollow stems of the rice plants act as tubes, the methane gas moves up from the soil and into the air.

Other Heat-Trapping Gases

Besides carbon dioxide and methane, there are other gases that add to the atmosphere's heat-trapping ability. Chlorofluorocarbons, usually called CFCs, are created synthetically for use in refrigerators, air conditioners, foam, and insulation products, as well as for propellants in spray cans. CFCs are up to sixteen thousand times more effective than carbon dioxide at absorbing heat, and they contribute about 20 to 25 percent of the total anthropogenic greenhouse gases. Scientific studies have also connected CFCs with rapid destruction of the ozone layer, a

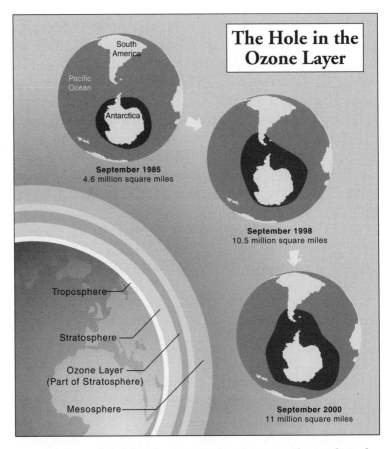

The Hole in the Ozone Layer

South America

Pacific Ocean

Antarctica

September 1985
4.6 million square miles

September 1998
10.5 million square miles

Troposphere

Stratosphere

Ozone Layer
(Part of Stratosphere)

Mesosphere

September 2000
11 million square miles

protective shield of atmospheric gas that absorbs harmful ultraviolet radiation from the sun. In most parts of the world, including the United States, CFCs are rarely used because of international control agreements. However, they have been in use all over the world for more than sixty years, and some countries still use them today. This is especially troublesome to scientists because CFCs remain in the atmosphere for at least one hundred years, and possibly two or three times longer.

Nitrous oxide is a powerful heat-trapping gas that is two hundred times more heat absorbent than CO_2 and constitutes about 9 percent of the total anthropogenic greenhouse gases. It is created when fossil fuels are burned, as well as from slash-and-burn agriculture. However, the main source of nitrous oxide is chemical fertilizers, which are usually made from nitrogen. When these fertilizers are spread on lawns or golf courses, parks or farm fields, nitrogen is released into the soil. Once it reacts with oxygen in the air, nitrous oxide is formed. In the past, nitrous oxide was not considered one of the primary heat-trapping gases. But like carbon dioxide and methane, atmospheric concentrations of nitrous oxide have continued to increase, and many scientists now believe it is a contributor to global warming.

The Uncertainty Lingers

For as long as there has been a planet Earth, there have been fluctuations in temperature and this will continue in the future. Solid evidence has proven this to be fact, and it is the one area where all scientists agree. Where they differ is over the issue of human activities—specifically, whether or not anthropogenic greenhouse gases are causing the earth to warm at an unnaturally fast pace, and how much this will affect future climatic conditions. Scientists who believe humans are to blame say the evidence speaks for itself—that in the past several hundred years, humans have altered the atmosphere so much that irreparable damage has been done. Somerville sums up why he and other scientists have made these conclusions:

> Climate has varied on every time scale to which we have any observational access. Ice ages come and go on time scales of tens of thousands of years, for example. . . . Climate changes. It changes on all time scales. What's different between our time and our grandparents' time is that now humankind, which has been a passive spectator at this great natural pageant, has become an actor and is up on the stage. And what we—all 6 billion of us—do can affect the climate.[20]

Chapter 4

Signs of a Warming Planet

Whether global warming is caused by nature, by humans, or a combination of both, there are visible changes to the planet because of it. Since the 1980s, when scientists first became concerned about global warming, they have observed shifts in weather, as well as alterations in the earth's oceans, massive ice formations, plants, and wildlife—and to some extent, all have been attributed to a planet that is becoming warmer. There is an ongoing debate among scientists about why these changes are occurring, and there is also disagreement about whether or not the changes are significant. However, the fact that they *are* occurring cannot be disputed because the evidence speaks for itself.

Rising Sea Waters

One result of global warming is a temperature increase in the earth's oceans, which cover nearly three-fourths of the surface of the planet. Because of their size and their dark-colored waters, oceans absorb a tremendous amount of energy from the sun. They are able to retain heat for decades or longer, which means they function as the "memory" of the earth's climate system.

Scientists at the NOAA and the Scripps Institute of Oceanography say that the world's oceans have warmed significantly over the past forty years. Temperature measurements have been taken from the surface of the water to a depth of more than nine thousand feet at sites in the Indian, Atlantic, and Pacific Oceans. From analyzing this data, NOAA scientists have concluded that the oceans have warmed at the same rate as the earth's surface temperatures. They also say that substantial temperature changes are occurring at much lower depths than they previously believed.

When oceans become warmer than normal, the water expands and becomes less dense, which causes it to spread and take up more of the planet's surface area. According to Curt Larsen, a scientist with the U.S. Geological Survey (USGS), worldwide sea levels are rising each year about twice as fast as normal. He explains how this affects one particular area, the Chesapeake Bay in Maryland, which has been the target of studies since the 1980s: "Let's say that 3 millimeters a year is an inch a decade. We are working on low-lying areas of Chesapeake Bay that have an elevation of three feet above sea level and the actual slope is very low. An inch may result in the loss of several thousand feet of marsh or lowlands. People don't think an inch a decade is very much, when in fact, it can be really significant."[21] Throughout both the Chesapeake and Delaware Bays, scientists are discovering that marshes cannot keep up with the rate of sea level rise. As a result, wetlands are becoming submerged and destroyed in those areas, as well as in other Atlantic coast states such as Florida and Georgia. Many beaches have been narrowed or completely submerged underwater as well.

Rising sea levels have affected the Atlantic coastline at Cape Hatteras, North Carolina. In 1870, when the Cape Hatteras Lighthouse was built, it stood 1,500 feet back from the shoreline. As sea waters continued to rise over the years, the coastline

North Carolina's Cape Hatteras Lighthouse was moved to save it from being washed away by rising ocean levels caused by global warming.

steadily became eroded and by 1987, the ocean had crept to within 160 feet of the lighthouse. North Carolina officials knew if they did not do something the historic treasure would be lost. In 1999, in an attempt to save the 2,800-ton lighthouse, it was moved more than a half mile from its original location.

Expanding ocean waters have affected coastal areas in other parts of the world. For example, rising seas have covered or are threatening low-lying Pacific islands such as Samoa and Fiji. The tiny island nation of Majuro, which is located about halfway between Hawaii and Australia, has lost about 20 percent of its beachfront in the past ten years. The same effects are also being seen in colder parts of the world, such as Alaska, where rising Arctic Sea waters are flooding native villages and towns. In

Barrow, Alaska, the northernmost city in the United States, it has become necessary for the entire population of forty-five hundred people to move because the town is gradually disappearing into the sea.

Destruction of Coral

In addition to rising sea levels, another risk of warming ocean waters is the destruction of coral reefs, which are extremely sensitive to temperature changes of any kind. The polyps that build coral reefs have clear bodies, but many tropical reefs are brilliantly colored because of algae cells, known as zooxanthellae, that live within the tissue of the coral polyps. The zooxanthellae provide the polyps with oxygen and food, and they also produce the pigment that creates the vivid reds, yellows, blues, and purples of the coral. When water temperatures become too high, the warmer water causes the polyps to expel zooxanthellae. Once the algae cells have been expelled, the white skeletons show through the

This coral has begun to bleach from a rise in the ocean's temperature. Pollution and intense light can also cause coral to bleach.

clear bodies of the polyps, and the coral takes on a bleached appearance. Coral bleaching can also be caused by conditions other than warmer waters, such as intense light and extreme pollution. Major bleaching, however, is usually associated with unusually high sea temperatures. If the water remains warm enough for the bleaching to persist for too long, this will cause the corals to die.

A June 1999 report by the World Wildlife Fund states that unusually high water temperatures have caused massive coral reef bleaching in recent years, most notably during 1997 and 1998. This occurred in most tropical regions, including the Pacific Ocean, Indian Ocean, Red Sea, Persian Gulf, Mediterranean Sea, and Caribbean Sea, where large numbers of coral turned completely white and died. In some parts of the Indian Ocean, more than 90 percent of the coral has been lost. All in all, an estimated 16 percent of the world's coral reefs were destroyed during 1998, and some of those species were up to seven hundred years old.

After 1999, the world's coral population continued to suffer from warmer ocean temperatures, and 2002 was the second worse year ever reported. One example of severe coral damage has occurred on Australia's Great Barrier Reef, which is considered one of the seven natural wonders of the world. Australian scientists report that coral bleaching was widespread on the Great Barrier Reef during 2002, when between 60 and 95 percent of the coral was severely damaged.

Melting Ice

Just as global warming causes ocean waters to warm, it is also causing changes in the world's ice formations. In the polar regions, huge sections of ice have thinned and broken off. One place this is happening is on the continent of Antarctica, where about 90 percent of the world's ice is found. Much of this ice is contained in ice shelves, or thick portions of ice

This satellite photo shows the pieces of the Larsen B ice shelf that broke off in 2002. Polar warming caused the ice to thin and break off.

sheets that are fed by glaciers. In February 2002, a massive Antarctic ice shelf called the Larsen B split apart and fell into the sea. Before it collapsed into small icebergs and fragments, the Larsen B was 650 feet thick and about the size of the state of Rhode Island. David Vaughan, a glaciologist with the British Antarctic Survey, says that because of the warming in the Antarctic Peninsula, his group had predicted that ice shelves would collapse—but they were not prepared for it to happen so fast. He explains: "Since [1998] warming on the peninsula has continued and we watched as piece-by-piece Larsen B has retreated. We knew what was left would collapse eventually, but the speed of it is staggering. Hard to believe that 500 billion [tons] of ice sheet has disintegrated in less than a month."[22]

At the opposite end of the world in the Arctic Sea, the ice covering has also been shrinking. The Arctic holds the second largest ice mass after Antarctica, and scientists studying the area say that ice sheets have been thinning for the past forty years. Using satellite measurements, scientists at the National Snow and Ice Data Center found that Arctic Sea ice in Greenland had shrunk by nearly three hundred thousand square miles—the largest decrease ever seen on the polar island.

It is not just ice sheets and glaciers in the world's coldest regions that are showing the effects of warmer global temperatures. According to the U.S. Environmental Protection Agency, the largest remaining glaciers at Glacier National Park in Montana are now only a third as large as they were in 1850. Plus, researchers have documented the rapid retreat of mountain glaciers in the Alps, the Himalayas, Ecuador, Venezuela, and New Guinea, among other areas. Since Lonnie Thompson has been exploring glaciers in the highest altitudes of the tropics, he has watched the ice continue to shrink. On Africa's Kilimanjaro, for example, there were about seven and a half square miles of ice in 1912. When Thompson photographed the ice in February 2000, he noted that the ice had shrunk to less than one and a half square miles—a loss of more than 80 percent. Plus, he has noted that ice is disappearing in Peru, another tropical area where he explores high-altitude glaciers. Peru's Quelccaya Glacier has shrunk by 20 percent since 1963, and there is now a lake that did not exist even as recently as 1974. Thompson says that in some areas, the ice is retreating at the rate of about one foot per day.

Effects on Wildlife

Crumbling ice has had a harmful effect on wildlife in regions throughout the world. Antarctica, for example, has a very large penguin population. In the past fifty years, temperatures on the Antarctic Peninsula have climbed much faster than in the rest of the world—and in that same period, the penguin population has seen a sharp decline. This was partly caused by the breakup of an enormous iceberg called the B15 in March 2000. Penguins have always been able to swim in the clear waters of the Ross Sea and hunt for krill, tiny shrimplike creatures that are their main source of food. After the iceberg split apart, massive chunks of ice blocked much of the Ross Sea. This meant the penguins had to walk, rather than swim, to and from their colonies. And since they walked more slowly than they could swim, the trip was much longer and many died of exhaustion. Female penguins that could not return to their nests were not able to feed their chicks, and so the young penguins did not survive.

Another result of the breakup of the B15 was its devastating effect on the Antarctic food chain. In the past, phytoplankton, or microscopic plants, thrived in the open water of the Ross Sea. These plants are considered the bottom of the food chain because they provide food for the krill eaten by various aquatic wildlife. Since the Ross Sea has become impeded by ice, phytoplankton has dropped by 40 percent because there is less open water where it can grow. This decrease in phytoplankton has led to a severe shortage of krill. As a result, thousands of penguins, seals, and seabirds have been unable to find food and have died of starvation.

The Arctic-dwelling polar bear is also a victim of changes in polar ice. In the Hudson Bay region of Canada, polar bears roam the ice hunting for food during the winter and early spring. During the summer when they cannot reach food, they fast. So, in the months when they are able to hunt, they must catch and eat enough to build ample amounts of fat on their bodies to sustain them during their fasting period. Over the past twenty years, warmer temperatures have caused Hudson Bay ice to break up three or four weeks earlier in the spring, which means the bears have less time to hunt. As a result, they have less food to hold them over for the winter so they lose weight—and when that happens, they are in grave danger of starving to death. Zoologist Ian Stirling has studied the Hudson Bay's polar bears for nearly twenty years, and he explains why the warming climate is having such an effect on them: "Some people have asked me why wouldn't they walk further north. The reason is there's already bears there. The other reason is that these bears grew up here, they know this area. They are committed to being here and if the ice just gets less and less and less . . . if the climate keeps on warming, ultimately there won't be polar bears in this part of the world."[23]

Vanishing Permafrost

When the climate warms enough in cold areas to cause ice to melt, permafrost—permanently frozen rock and soil—is also affected. Permafrost is located

Polar bear cubs play near Canada's Hudson Bay. Global warming now melts the frozen bay earlier in the year, reducing the amount of time the bears have to hunt.

in regions that have very cold climates all year long, and it underlies more than 50 percent of Russia and Canada and most of Antarctica. Depending on the region and the climate, permafrost can be hundreds or even thousands of feet thick. In areas such as Alaska and Siberia, where permafrost covers more than 85 percent of the land, most buildings, roads, airfields, bridges, railroad tracks, and even entire cities and towns are built on permafrost foundations. When temperatures become warmer than normal, the solid, frozen ground thaws and becomes a soggy, icy, swamplike surface.

In Alaska—where temperatures have risen as much as seven degrees higher than normal—nearly the entire state has been hard-hit because of thawing permafrost. In cities and towns all over the state, melting permafrost is causing the ground to shift and become increasingly unstable as it develops holes, pits, and trenches. As a result, homes and other buildings are damaged or destroyed, roads become as bumpy as roller coasters, and airport runways and railroad tracks have buckled. In the summer of 2002 a sinkhole, or collapsed section of land, developed along a highway, and a hundred feet of earth was suddenly flushed away. According to George Levasseur, who works for the Alaska Department of Transportation, forty-five miles of highway had to be rebuilt in hundreds of different locations, and the repairs cost more than $4 million. He describes the magnitude of the problem: "The whole Alaska Highway from Northway to the border is coming apart. It's just exploding."[24] The shifting earth causes erosion and landslides, as well as the collapse of large sections of forestland—which kills trees and all other vegetation growing there. The moving land causes silt and gravel to be dumped into rivers and creeks, which creates floods and damages bridges.

In the Alaskan coastal village of Kipnuk, most structures show signs that the ground beneath them

Global warming is responsible for very destructive storms. This huge sinkhole resulted from large amounts of rain during a severe storm in Shoreline, Washington.

is highly unstable and residents fear that their entire town is sinking. Roads are damaged and buildings are tilting, as one school principal reported: "If you put a marble on the floor, in one year it'll roll in one direction; in the next year it'll go in the other direction."[25]

Across the Alaskan border in the Yukon Territory of northwestern Canada, melting permafrost is causing serious problems for the Inuvialuit, a native people whose ancestors settled on Herschel Island many generations ago. Because the earth is no longer frozen, coffins, long buried in the island's graveyards, are working their way to the surface, as one writer explains: "Graves are pushing up from the ground as the ice within the carpet of permafrost melts, churning the soil beneath it into a muddy soup, spitting up foreign contents, sending whole hill slopes sliding downward. On a far tip of this island an entire grave site one day got up and slipped into the sea."[26]

Violent Weather

Warmer climates can also influence the weather. Scientists cannot say for sure that global warming causes extreme weather, but they do know that weather at its hottest typically breeds the most severe storms. Powerful thunderstorms, hurricanes, and tornadoes are naturally created when warm air rises and collides with extremely cold air high in the atmosphere. The hotter the air, the faster it rises, and the stronger its clash with the cold air. So, the storms that are created are much more fierce.

The intensity of storms is also affected by the warming ocean waters. As the earth becomes warmer, the ocean heats up, causing storms such as cyclones and hurricanes to be especially severe. Science historian and author Angela Eiss explains this: "The problem . . . is that the higher the overall temperature, the greater the intensity of all cyclones. . . . [T]he temperature sets the maximum intensity a storm can reach. . . . So, if you increase the temperature, you increase the intensities of all tropical storms—just as a rising tide raises all the boats."[27]

Hurricanes, a particularly violent kind of storm, are only formed over oceans because they draw their energy from warm tropical waters, normally above eighty-one degrees Fahrenheit. The World Wildlife Fund explains how this is connected to a warmer climate: "Once this temperature is reached, so much water evaporates from the sea surface that, as it condenses, sufficient energy is released to create a 'vortex' around which the hurricane forms. Every degree above that temperature produces an exponential increase in the [potential] for storms."[28] After a hurricane develops, it gathers heat and energy through contact with warm ocean waters. As the ocean continues to contribute more moisture to the storm, the hurricane becomes as powerful as a gigantic heat engine, with winds of more than 155 miles per hour.

Hurricanes can last for days or even weeks, and they usually cover thousands of miles of land before they die out. Between 1995 and 1998, there were thirty-three hurricanes reported—an all-time record. In 1998, the hottest year on record, there were four Atlantic hurricanes in progress at one time. Scientists say that in a hundred years of observations, that had never occurred before. In the fall of that same year, the deadliest Atlantic hurricane in more than two hundred years—Hurricane Mitch—struck Central America. Before it had run its course, the hurricane had killed more than eleven hundred people, left millions of others homeless, and caused billions of dollars in damage. In Nicaragua, Hurricane Mitch caused mudslides that buried whole villages; and in Honduras, raging floods caused by the storm swept away bridges and devastated crops.

Hurricane Mitch devastated this Honduran city and much of Central America in 1998. Rising seawater temperatures increase the incidence and violence of hurricanes.

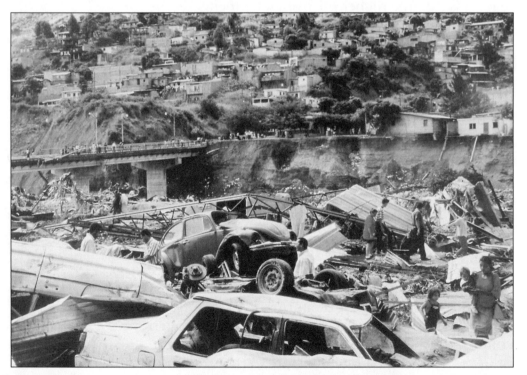

What Is Next?

Even though scientists agree that the earth is showing the effects of a warming climate, they do not
agree about what that means now, or what it could
mean in the future. Robert B. Gagosian says it is crucial for scientists to learn everything they can about
global warming. He explains:

> In just the past year, we have seen ominous
> signs that we may be headed toward a poten-
> tially dangerous threshold. If we cross it, Earth's
> climate could switch gears and jump very
> rapidly—not gradually—into a completely dif-
> ferent mode of operation. This is not something
> new under the Sun. It has happened throughout
> Earth's history, and it could happen again. . . .
> As a society, I believe we must face the potential
> for abrupt climate change. Perhaps we can miti-
> gate the changes. If not, at least we can still take
> steps to adapt to them. . . . In other words, the
> more knowledge we have—the more reliably we
> can predict changes—the better our chances.
> Maybe over the edge of the cliff, there's just a
> three-inch drop-off. Or maybe there's a big,
> fluffy bed full of pillows. My worry is that we
> are indeed approaching this cliff blindfolded.[29]

Chapter 5

Global Warming and the Future

Oone of the main points of contention among scientists is what will happen to the planet as a result of global warming. Some believe that the earth will actually benefit if the climate continues to grow warmer. Others insist that the opposite is true, saying that if the planet continues to heat up, the effects will be catastrophic. NASA sums up these very different perspectives:

> Many see [global warming] as a harbinger of what is to come. If we don't curb our greenhouse gas emissions, then low-lying nations could be awash in seawater, rain and drought patterns across the world could change, hurricanes could become more frequent. . . . On the other hand, there are those, some of whom are scientists, who believe that global warming will result in little more than warmer winters and increased plant growth. They point to the flaws in scientists' measurements, the complexity of the climate, and the uncertainty in the climate models used to predict climate change. They claim that attempting to lower greenhouse emissions may do more damage to the world economy and human society than any amount of global warming. In truth, the future probably fits somewhere between these two scenarios.[30]

How Predictions Are Made

The climate models to which NASA refers are powerful computer programs used to simulate climate and predict future climate changes. Models can be used to simulate temperature changes that occur from both natural and anthropogenic causes. Scientists enter data on different conditions, such as atmospheric concentrations of greenhouse gases, ocean currents, cloud cover, energy from the sun, and ocean circulation, as well as others. Then, as they change and adjust the variables, they can simulate what might happen when actual climate conditions change. NASA compares climate models to the computer programs used by detectives to envision what

This illustration mimics a computer model used to predict climate change. The melting earth suggests global warming is a serious threat.

A scientist explains a general circulation model generated by a supercomputer. Scientists debate the value of computer model predictions.

missing persons would look like years after their disappearance. In the same way the detective programs are constructed on information about people's faces, climate models are constructed based on data that relate to the earth's climate.

There are many different types of climate models. The simplest models can be run on personal computers, and are designed to focus on one particular time frame, or to investigate a specific phenomenon. The most sophisticated climate models are supercomputers known as general circulation models (GCMs). Climate models have evolved from the same sort of computer programs that are used to make weather forecasts. Richard C.J. Somerville says that just as people criticize meteorologists when weather predictions are wrong, some global warming skeptics denounce climate models as useless—and he insists that is not true. He also says that just as weather simulation programs have improved markedly over time, climate models are also being improved and perfected. He shares his perspective about their use for predicting a future climate: "The model in the end is a computer program. We can't take the atmosphere or the whole planet and put it in a test tube and do experiments on it. So instead, we simulate it in a computer. That's turned out to be the best way of incorporating all the various complexities."[31]

The Doubtful Scientists

Climate prediction is not an exact science, and no one who uses climate models will say that they are perfect. S. Fred Singer is highly skeptical about the ability of climate models to accurately predict future climates. He bases his belief on the fact that the predictions of models do not always agree with what is actually happening with the climate. He says, for instance, that current models show that the climate should be warming by one degree Fahrenheit per decade, in the middle troposphere, but that is not what observations actually show. Singer explains his opinion about these models: "Until the observations and the models agree, or until one or the other is resolved, it's very difficult for people—and for myself, of course—to believe in the predictive power of the current models. Now, the models are getting better. And perhaps in ten years we will have models that can be trusted, that is, that agree with actual observations."[32]

Richard S. Lindzen is another scientist who is skeptical about the effectiveness of climate models. He has often stated his belief that the models are merely experimental tools with questionable value. Lindzen feels that computer predictions should be viewed only as possibilities—not facts—yet he says this is not often the case and he shares his thoughts about why: "Unfortunately, there is a tendency to hold in awe anything that emerges from a sufficiently large computer. There is also a reluctance on the part of many modellers to admit to the experimental nature of their models lest public support for their efforts diminish."[33]

Could Global Warming Be a Benefit?

Just as Singer, Lindzen, and some other scientists are skeptical about the effectiveness of computer models, they also doubt the scientists who believe that global warming will be harmful for the planet. They base their beliefs on the fact that there has never been a time in history when the earth did not experience widely fluctuating temperatures. Humans, animals, and plant life have always adapted to changing conditions, and these scientists believe this will continue to happen. Plus, because carbon dioxide is necessary for the survival of all living things, their perspective is that the more CO_2 there is in the atmosphere, the more the planet—and its inhabitants—will benefit.

Drs. Craig D. Idso and Keith E. Idso, from the Center for the Study of Carbon Dioxide and Global Change, say that excess carbon dioxide in the atmosphere will have nothing but positive results. They believe that the United States should not be criticized for the amount of CO_2 it is adding to the atmosphere, as they explain:

> The United States should be *applauded* for its emissions of CO_2; for it is the ongoing rise in the air's CO_2 content that will ultimately prove the salvation of the planet. How do we know that? Because carbon dioxide is the very *elixir of life;* the primary raw material upon which nearly all plant life—and, hence, nearly all animal life (including man!)—depends for its existence. And the more CO_2 there is in the air, the better plants grow; and, consequently, the more food there is for human and animal consumption.[34]

Dr. Thomas Gale Moore, an economist at Stanford University's Hoover Institution, agrees with this perspective. Moore says that virtually all plants will thrive in an environment where there is an abundance of carbon dioxide. He believes that global warming will bring shorter winters, which would mean longer growing seasons for crops. Also, winters would be warmer, so according to Moore, there would be more affordable heating bills, less ice and snow to hinder drivers, and fewer airline delays because of bad weather. He sums up his thoughts: "Pundits, politicians and the press have argued that global warming will bring disaster to the world, but there are good reasons to believe that, if it occurs, we will like it. Where do retirees go when they are free to move? Certainly not to Duluth [Minnesota]. People like warmth. When weather reporters on TV say, 'it will be a great day,' they usually mean that it will be warmer than normal."[35]

Some scientists argue that just as flowers thrive in a greenhouse, plants around the world will flourish in a warmer climate with more carbon dioxide.

"Unknown Territory"

Scientists do not dispute the fact that plant life thrives on carbon dioxide. What they disagree about is how much is too much. Many believe that the amount of CO_2 and other greenhouse gases that humans are adding to the atmosphere go far beyond what the planet can handle. This is the viewpoint of Dr. Tom Wigley, a climatologist and senior scientist with the National Center for Atmospheric Research. He acknowledges that not all global warming is harmful nor is an increase in CO_2 necessarily bad, because carbon dioxide accelerates plant growth. Wigley explains what does concern him: "What we're afraid of is that if the planet warms too much, we're going into unknown territory. We can't predict the climate well enough to know what to expect. So we certainly don't want to go too far down the road, down the pathway of global warming. We have time to think about what to do. But eventually, we have to do something dramatic."[36]

Tom Crowley, a climate researcher in the oceanography department at Texas A&M, is another scientist who is concerned about the earth's future because so much is still unknown. There was a time when he was doubtful about the existence of global warming but that time has passed, as he explains: "To me the question of whether global warming is happening is receding as the central question. In my view, it's already here—and I didn't believe that two years ago. Now the question is: How will it affect us?"[37]

Dire Predictions

Scientists who are the most alarmed about global warming predict that the earth is headed for catastrophe if the temperature keeps rising—which they are convinced it will continue to do. They know that greenhouse gases, such as carbon dioxide, have been building up for several hundred years. Once they are in the atmosphere, most of them remain there for a very long time, and billions of tons of these gases are still being emitted every year. Also, over the past fifty years the planet warmed more rapidly than at any other time in history. Many scientists are convinced that temperatures will continue to rise at the same rate—or perhaps even faster. Dr. Henry Jacoby of the Massachusetts Institute of Technology (MIT) says that even though scientists cannot be sure how serious global warming is, there are reasons to be concerned about the future and he explains why:

The potential is that it might be quite serious. That is, the change in climate, temperature, and rainfall . . . the potential for changes in storminess, extreme events like droughts and floods . . . the potential over the century is substantial. We don't know [for sure], but the potential is there. And since we're building up this stock of

This drawing depicts how the world will heat up as a result of greenhouse gases trapped in the atmosphere.

greenhouse gases in the atmosphere and they don't go away fast, it makes a big difference when you start to deal with it.[38]

One group that has issued a strong warning is the Intergovernmental Panel on Climate Change (IPCC), which is composed of scientists from all over the world. Since 1988, the IPCC has studied the global climate including why it changes, different factors that influence those changes, how a warming climate will affect living things and the environment, and what can be done to stop it. In March 2001, the IPCC concluded that most of the warming during the past fifty years has been caused by human activities. The group also projected that by the year 2100, the earth's average surface temperature will have increased between 2.5 degrees and 10.4 degrees Fahrenheit from 1990 temperature readings.

Scientists from the Intergovernmental Panel on Climate Change (IPCC) warn of the dire consequences of global warming at a 2001 news conference.

Some occurrences such as warming ocean waters, disappearing sea ice, melting permafrost, and extreme weather are already happening—and as the climate continues to grow warmer, the IPCC warns that these phenomena will become much worse. For instance, the group projects that in the next hundred years more than 50 percent of the world's glaciers will disappear, and sea levels will rise between 3.5 to 34 inches. If that happens, the result will be erosion of coastlines, destruction of wetlands, and severe flooding. Because as much as 50 percent of the world's population lives in coastal communities, floods could force millions of people to abandon their homes.

NASA offers a more conservative prediction about ocean waters, saying that although sea levels are likely to rise, the results will be nothing like those dramatized in movies: "The Statue of Liberty won't be up to her neck in water, and we won't all be living on flotillas on an endless sea. . . . The rise will mainly be due to seawater expanding from the increased ocean temperatures and run-off from the melting of continental glaciers and a slight melting of the Greenland Ice Sheet."[39] NASA says that for the most part, ice sheets in Antarctica will probably stay in place, and may even grow because of increased precipitation over the next century. The agency adds, however, that if global warming caused unusually rapid melting of polar ice sheets, sea levels would rise dramatically.

Altering the Ecosystem

Even though NASA scientists say that higher levels of carbon dioxide would benefit some plant life, they caution that most changes caused by increased CO_2 will likely be for the worst. If a steadily warming planet leads to the flooding of coastal wetlands, countless species of fish and birds would be driven out, and many types of wetland vegetation would

A satellite photograph reveals that these ice sheets in the Bering Sea are melting due to global warming. Many scientists predict that climate changes will affect all life on Earth.

die. Also, whenever natural habitats change, the species that live in them must change along with them. That means as the earth becomes warmer, plants and animals that cannot cope with the warmer climate conditions must migrate somewhere else—and if they cannot migrate fast enough, they will not survive.

John Firor explains how continued global warming would affect the world's forests:

> By studying the last ice age, we know that forests in the eastern U.S. migrated northward as the weather warmed. . . . Some who study the impacts of climate change note that these forests migrated at what seems like a rapid pace—but the climate changes we are now forcing on the Earth because of greenhouse gases are happening many times faster than the changes from the ice age. What that means is that forests will probably not be able to migrate fast enough to reproduce, so they will be lost.[40]

Stephen H. Schneider shares Firor's views. He offers his thoughts about what a warming planet could mean:

> How are the species of trees . . . and birds and so forth . . . going to migrate? In history, they just migrated. Now they have to cross factories, farms, freeways, and urban settlements. So if you have the combination of fragmented habitats with nature getting into smaller and smaller patches, now you change the climate ten times faster than the history for which they have experience, this seems to me an absolute prescription for an extinction crisis where we lose a large fraction of the species now on earth.[41]

Just as plant and animal species may not be able to migrate fast enough to survive, those that live in the world's oceans and lakes may not be able to tolerate water that is warmer than normal. For instance, many fish species are highly sensitive to temperature changes; and when the changes are extreme, the fish can die. In addition, if the oceans continue to warm, the production of phytoplankton would be reduced—and that could have a devastating effect on the entire food chain. There have been major declines in populations of Alaskan salmon and other types of fish, as well as seabirds and marine mammals, and some scientists believe this is a direct result of the depleting supply of phytoplankton.

Risks for Humans

Wildlife and plants are not the only living things that could have a difficult time adapting if the average global climate became warmer. It could also cause severe problems for human beings. One possible result of a warmer global climate would be an increase in heat waves. This phenomenon could potentially affect every region of the world; but it would be especially devastating to people in Africa and Asia where average year-round temperatures are already extremely hot. Many countries such as Afghanistan, Ethiopia, and India have large populations. Because they also have high poverty rates, these people are particularly vulnerable to heat waves and droughts. According to the Union of Concerned Scientists, residents of these areas are already suffering as a result of rising temperatures. For example, extensive fires affected people along the west coast of South Africa during January 2000, and during 2001 Kenya suffered from the worst drought in sixty years. The group also cites a May 2002 heat wave in southern India that resulted in the highest one-week death toll ever recorded.

Higher temperatures can also subject human beings to increased outbreaks of deadly infectious diseases such as malaria, dengue fever, and encephali-

An Indian rickshaw driver naps in the shade to escape a heat wave in Calcutta in 2002. Tropical areas may suffer most from global warming.

tis. This is because a warmer climate can lead to an increase in mosquitoes, which carry the diseases. IPCC scientists say that as warmer temperatures continue spreading north and south from the tropics, disease-carrying mosquitoes will follow, putting increasing numbers of people all over the world at risk.

Scientific Speculation

No matter where scientists stand on the global warming issue, they all have strong opinions about it. Some believe that more carbon dioxide and warmer temperatures will be good for the planet, while others believe that the future holds great harm. At this point, there is more guesswork involved than anything else—something even the most astute scientists do not deny. Schneider says that many people think of the study of global warming as a fuzzy, uncertain science, which, in many ways, it is. He believes, however, that even though there are still many doubts about global warming, the potential is serious enough that it warrants attention, as he explains: "The dilemma rests, metaphorically, in our need to gaze into a very dirty crystal ball; but the tough judgment to be made here is precisely how long we should clean the glass before acting on what we believe we see inside."[42]

Chapter 6

A Cooler Earth

Although most scientists agree that humans have in some way influenced climate change, whether humans should try to stop global warming is one of the most hotly debated topics in the scientific world. In fact, of all the points about which scientists disagree on the global warming issue, a possible solution seems to spark the fiercest debate. Some say that the planet is more robust than fragile—that it has always managed to maintain the right balance in the past, and it will naturally correct itself in the future. Others, however, insist that since people have caused warming, people must take corrective measures to stop it.

Cutting Back on Fossil Fuels

The scientists who are most alarmed about global warming insist that in order to fix it, the burning of fossil fuels must be dramatically cut back. This would not make an immediate difference because heat-trapping gases such as carbon dioxide and methane will remain in the atmosphere for many years. But if steps were taken now to reduce emissions, the gases would eventually begin to diminish and the rate of global warming would slow.

However, that would be anything but simple because fossil fuels are used by people all over the world. Petroleum products furnish power for all different kinds of transportation. Oil and natural gas are used to heat homes, stores, and office buildings, as well as everything from small businesses to multimillion-dollar corporations. Coal is burned to operate water treatment plants, and to run power plants that generate much of the world's electricity. If fossil fuel use were suddenly cut, it would require people to make major changes in their lives.

Some scientists warn that reducing the use of fossil fuels would cause great financial hardship. This is especially true in the United States because America's economy is more dependent on fossil fuels than that of other countries. Since economic growth depends on energy, scientists such as Fred Singer believe that any move to restrict the use of coal—the cheapest fuel available—could cause electricity prices to skyrocket. Singer explains his perspective about cutting back on fossil fuels:

> I'm not a great believer in buying insurance if the risks are small and the premiums are high. Nobody in his right mind would do that. But

Gasoline-fueled automobiles create much of the pollution that causes global warming. Reducing the use of fossil fuels can slow global warming.

this is the case here. We're being asked to buy an insurance policy against a risk that is very small, if at all, and pay a very heavy premium. We're being asked to reduce energy use, not just by a few percent but . . . by about 35 percent within ten years. That means giving up one-third of all energy use, using one-third less electricity, throwing out one-third of all cars, perhaps . . . it would hit people very hard, particularly people who can least afford it.[43]

Like Singer, Thomas Gale Moore believes that the cost of doing away with fossil fuels would be too high of a price for people to pay. He explains: "Let's not rush into costly programs to stave off something that we may like if it occurs. Warmer is better, richer is healthier; acting now is foolish."[44]

Other scientists, however, believe that the cost of reducing fossil fuels will be much lower than people think. Studies done by the U.S. Department of Energy show that the United States could reduce its CO_2 emissions at a low cost, and perhaps even save money in the long term. John J. Berger believes that the claims sometimes made about high costs are untrue or exaggerated. He says that an effort to reduce dependence on fossil fuels could actually stimulate the economy and vastly improve the planet. He shares his thoughts on how the planet—and also the world economy—would benefit by cutting back on fossil fuel use: "Lakes and streams would sparkle. . . . The threat of global climate change due to human activities would vanish. The U.S. would go from being the world's major cause of global warming to being the world's premier source of clean energy systems [renewable energy]."[45] Berger points out that if the world reduced its dependence on fossil fuels, the environment would be cleaner, the quality of life would be improved, and people would save money on energy costs.

Too High a Price?

Scientists who are in favor of cutting back on the use of fossil fuels are the first to say that it will not be easy and it will take time. Stephen H. Schneider says that the world cannot turn off its dependence on carbon-based energy overnight, but that steps must be taken now to move away from fossil fuels. He believes one possible solution is to charge higher prices for carbon-based fuels, as he explains: "If we had a price on carbon, if we weren't all allowed to use the atmosphere as a free sewer, then the inventive genius of our industrial folks . . . to invent non-carbon-based alternatives would be stimulated. As long as the price of energy remains so that a bottle of mineral water at the store costs three times more per gallon than gasoline at the pump, we haven't got incentives for that kind of development."[46]

The Union of Concerned Scientists also believes that corrective measures, such as enacting CO_2 emission laws, must be taken now or the planet will suffer permanent damage. The group says that by waiting ten or twenty years, or longer, before taking action, global warming will be much more difficult to address and the problems will be more serious, as they describe:

> We're treating our atmosphere like we once did our rivers. We used to dump waste thoughtlessly into our waterways. . . . But when entire fisheries were poisoned and rivers began to catch fire, we realized what a horrible mistake that was. Our atmosphere has limits too. CO_2 remains in the atmosphere for about 100 years. The longer we keep polluting, the longer it will take to recover and the more irreversible damage will be done.[47]

The word *polluting* is at the center of many scientific debates on global warming. Those who believe that the planet would benefit from higher levels of

An environmentalist group posted this sign on a California beach to protest pollution.

CO_2 do not believe the gas is a pollutant. So, they are very much against governmental policy that would place limits on CO_2 emissions. Fred Palmer, president of Western Fuels Association, agrees with the scientists who say that CO_2 is not a pollutant, as he explains:

> In the past, we've had these great struggles over pollution in the United States. Sulphur dioxide is a pollutant. . . . Carbon dioxide is a benign gas required for life on earth. It is not a pollutant. It is not regulated. There are no state laws dealing with CO_2. There are no Congressional laws that give any agency the right to regulate based on CO_2. So when the environmental community gets their hands on our policy apparatus in the U.S. and says, "we have to put less greenhouse gases in the atmosphere," they come first to us [the coal producers], because we are not only the biggest source of carbon dioxide, we're the biggest source of electricity.[48]

Green Companies

Even in the absence of government regulation of CO_2 emissions, a growing number of companies have taken action on their own by setting tough environmental standards for themselves. One example is the Business Environmental Leadership Council (BELC), which was formed to address the problems of global climate change. The group is composed of large oil, gas, chemical, and utility companies that are all committed to adopting environmentally sound technologies, as well as developing better ways to produce energy. Some BELC members include IBM, Intel, Boeing, Alcoa, American Electric Power, DuPont, Whirlpool, Shell International, Sunoco, Lockheed Martin, Toyota, Hewlett-Packard, DTE Energy, Georgia-Pacific, and BP Amoco, among others. Each company sets its own goals for reducing greenhouse gas emissions, and each monitors its own progress.

For instance, DuPont's goal for the year 2010 is to reduce emissions by 65 percent from 1990 levels. Holcium, a large cement manufacturer, vowed to reduce its emissions by 12 percent per ton of product manufactured between 2000 and 2008. BP Amoco has achieved its goal of reducing emissions by 10 percent from 1990 levels, and its target for the future is not to exceed these levels through the year 2012. Shell International's goal for 2002 was to reduce emissions by 10 percent, and the company beat that goal. Shell's commitment to help stop global warming is stated on its website as follows: "The Royal Dutch/Shell Group of Companies shares the widespread concern that the emission of greenhouse gases from human activities is leading to changes in the global climate. We believe action is required now to lay the foundation for eventually stabilizing greenhouse gas concentrations in the atmosphere in an equitable and an economically responsible way."[49]

A Windy Solution

Some members of the BELC are also committed to developing technologies that focus on renewable resources—resources that cannot be used up. In December 2002, BP Amoco announced the start-up of a wind farm in the Netherlands that will generate enough electricity for about twenty thousand Dutch households, without adding a trace of carbon dioxide or other greenhouse gases to the atmosphere.

As an energy source wind power is cheap to produce, pollution free, and readily available. Throughout history, wind power has been used for everything from powering ships to grinding grain, although its popularity waned as new kinds of technology developed. Now, however, according to Berger, wind power is growing faster than any other energy technology in the world. Much of that growth has been in Europe, but in March 2002, the U.S. Department of Energy announced a program called Wind Powering America. The organization's goal is to significantly increase the nation's use of wind energy by the year 2010.

Windmills like these are used to produce electricity. Wind power is clean and renewable.

Hydropower

Another renewable resource is hydropower—power generated through the use of flowing water. The most common type of hydropower plant uses a dam on a river or stream to capture water and store it in a reservoir. As water is released from the reservoir it flows through a turbine, causing the turbine to spin, which activates a generator that produces electricity. Not all hydropower plants require dams, though. Instead some, such as most hydropower plants in Hawaii, use small canals to channel river water through a turbine.

Like wind power, hydropower is a clean, nonpolluting energy resource. Currently, about 20 percent of the world's electricity is generated through the use of water; and in the United States, hydropower generates about 10 percent of the nation's electricity. There are some environmental concerns associated with hydropower because building new dams to restrict the flow of rivers or streams can alter natural habitats and disturb aquatic plants and wildlife. However, Berger says that existing capacity for hydropower can be expanded without having to construct new dams, as he explains: "Upgrading dams, by adding new turbines or rewinding old ones, could thus increase hydroelectric power generation by twenty-five percent, at relatively little cost, and it also might present opportunities for improving fish passage, downstream aquatic habitats, and water quality."[50]

Drawing Energy from the Sun

Just as there is energy potential in the earth's water, there is also great potential in sunlight because the sun emits such an enormous amount of energy. Scientists say that there is enough energy in twenty days of sunshine to equal the total energy stored in the earth's reserves of coal, oil, and natural gas.

Solar technologies harness the sun's energy and use it to provide utilities for businesses, industries, and homes. One product, called a concentrating solar system, for example, uses reflective materials such as mirrors to collect and focus the sun's heat, which then runs generators to produce electricity. Passive solar heating, cooling, and daylighting systems capture solar energy that heats and cools buildings, as well as providing a natural source of light. Solar hot water systems use the sun's energy to heat water. Photovoltaic solar cells, which convert sunlight directly into electricity, are most often used in calculators, watches, and to power outdoor light fixtures. More complex photovoltaic systems have the ability to light houses and other buildings.

Tapping the Earth's Core

Not only is there a tremendous amount of energy available from the sky above, there is also a vast store of energy buried deep in the ground. The production of geothermal energy takes advantage of that by tapping into the ancient heat of the earth's core. This heat is found at several different levels: in shallow reservoirs of hot water and steam; as hot, dry rock found deeper in the earth; and at the planet's deepest levels as molten rock.

Like sunlight, geothermal energy can be used to produce electricity. Unlike traditional power plants, geothermal power plants obtain steam to rotate turbines from a direct source found several miles below the surface of the planet. There are two kinds of geothermal power plants: dry steam plants, which pipe steam from underground wells; and flash steam plants, which convert geothermal reservoirs of hot water into steam, and then inject the unused water back into the reservoir.

There are other uses for geothermal energy besides creating steam. For example, in the western continental United States, as well as in Alaska and Hawaii, geothermal energy is used to provide heat directly to homes and businesses. Wells are drilled into geother-

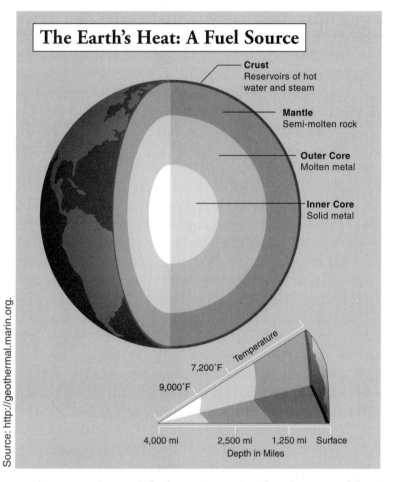

The Earth's Heat: A Fuel Source

Crust
Reservoirs of hot
water and steam

Mantle
Semi-molten rock

Outer Core
Molten metal

Inner Core
Solid metal

Temperature

7,200°F

9,000°F

4,000 mi   2,500 mi   1,250 mi   Surface
Depth in Miles

mal reservoirs until there is a steady stream of hot water, which is drawn up through the well. Then, a mechanical system delivers the hot water for such uses as heating buildings, raising plants in greenhouses, or drying crops.

Making Waste Materials Count

Another kind of renewable energy that has tremendous potential is biomass energy, produced from organic matter. Biomass energy makes use of waste materials generated by manufacturing, agriculture, and forestry, as well as common household garbage and sewage. One use for biomass is the generation of electricity. Waste materials are burned to produce steam that is captured by a turbine, and then a generator converts the steam into electricity. In some industries, the steam is also used for manufacturing processes or to heat buildings. For example, wood waste is often used to produce both electricity and steam at paper mills.

Another way that biomass can be used as an energy source is by recycling the methane that is emitted at landfills when organic waste materials decompose. Wells can be drilled in the landfills to release the methane from the layers of decaying matter, and then pipes from the wells carry the gas to a central point where it is filtered and cleaned before burning. One facility in Texas uses this process to generate enough electricity to power more than sixty-five hundred homes.

Because biomass can be converted to ethanol and methanol—liquid fuels that add no carbon dioxide to the air—its use could greatly reduce greenhouse gas emissions. Unlike other renewable energy sources, biomass can be converted directly into liquid fuels, called biofuels, which can be used to run cars, trucks, buses, airplanes, and trains. Many scientists believe that fuels made from biomass could go a long way toward meeting the transportation needs of the world.

Energy from Hydrogen

Another energy source that can produce fuel for the world's transportation needs is hydrogen, the most plentiful element in the universe. Hydrogen can produce electricity, heat, or synthetic chemicals. One of hydrogen's most valuable benefits is that when it is burned in an engine, it is virtually pollution-free.

Most hydrogen is currently made from natural gas, by using steam to separate the hydrocarbons from the gas. Another way of producing hydrogen uses an electrical current to separate water into its components of oxygen and hydrogen, in a process called electrolysis. Since the 1970s, NASA has used liquid hydrogen to propel the space shuttle and other rockets into orbit. Hydrogen fuel cells power the shuttle's electrical systems, producing a clean byproduct—pure water—that the crew is able to drink. Fuel cells, which are often compared to batteries, combine hydrogen and oxygen to produce electricity, heat, and water. Scientists consider them one of the most promising technologies for the world's future energy needs.

The Debate That Will Not Go Away

There are no simple answers to the global warming debate. As far back as the nineteenth century, when Svante Arrhenius first proposed his theory about carbon dioxide in the atmosphere, global warming has

The space shuttle, shown here during launch, uses clean-burning hydrogen for fuel. Hydrogen fuel technology may solve the world's future energy needs.

been a controversial scientific issue. Back then, only a handful of scientists agreed that humans had the capability to alter the earth's climate, while most thought the idea was nonsense. As time passed, however, more scientists became convinced that there was a definite connection between human activities and the steadily rising temperature of the earth—yet today the debate continues to rage on. Unlike some environmental issues, most of the controversy stems from a lack of definitive proof that human actions are causing the earth to warm. When ice sheets melt and oceans rise and hurricanes happen with greater frequency, some scientists insist that humans are to blame—while others say those things are nothing more than products of nature.

Patrick J. Michaels says there have been times in the past when environmental predictions were proven wrong, and he believes that global warming is the same type of issue, as he explains: "We've been throwing increasing amounts of money at this problem for years now and the fact of the matter is that we still can't tell, literally, which way is up when it comes to climate change."[51] In a separate article, Michaels, along with two other authors, writes there is no mechanism that can stop global warming in the near future because what the future holds is unknown. He also says the more serious question provoked by what is known about global warming is this one: "Is the way the planet warms something that we should even try to stop?"[52]

Schneider believes that it definitely is the responsibility of humans to stop global warming, and he says measures must be taken now because time is running out for the planet: "The only way to prove it for sure is hang around 10, 20, or 30 more years, when the evidence would be overwhelming. But in the meantime, we're conducting a global experiment. And we're all in the test tube."[53]

Notes

Introduction: The Warming of the Earth

1. John Weier, "Global Warming," NASA, April 8, 2002. www.nasa.gov.
2. John J. Berger, *Beating the Heat: Why and How We Must Combat Global Warming.* Berkeley, CA: Berkeley Hills Books, 2000, p. 13.

Chapter 1: What Is Global Warming?

3. Quoted in PBS, *What's Up with the Weather?* December 30, 1999. www.pbs.org.
4. National Oceanic and Atmospheric Administration (NOAA), *Paleoclimatology Program.* www.ngdc.noaa.gov.
5. Robert B. Gagosian, "Triggering Abrupt Climate Change: Can Global Warming Cause an 'Ice Age'?," *What's New?,* Woods Hole Oceanographic Institute. www.whoi.edu.
6. William Hutton, "Scientists, in Their Own Words," *The Hutton Commentaries*, February, 1, 2001. www.hutton commentaries.com.
7. Wallace S. Broecker, Lamont-Doherty Earth Observatory, Columbia University. www.ldeo.columbia.edu.

Chapter 2: The Study of Climate Change

8. Gagosian, "Triggering Abrupt Climate Change."
9. National Oceanic and Atmospheric Administration, *Paleoclimatology Program.*
10. Quoted in CNN, "Deciphering the Ice," *America's Best Society and Culture,* 2001. www.cnn.com.
11. Quoted in PBS. *What's Up with the Weather?*
12. Dr. John Firor, interview with the author, December 12, 2002.
13. NASA, "About the Terra Spacecraft," *Terra: The Earth Observing System (EOS) Flagship.* http://terra.nasa.gov.

Chapter 3: The Human Contribution

14. Stephen H. Schneider, *Global Warming: Are We Entering the Greenhouse Century?,* San Francisco: Sierra Club Books, 1989, p. 65.

15. Quoted in PBS, *What's Up with the Weather?*
16. Gale Christianson, "From Benevolence to Menace: An Historian's Biography of Global Warming," *Earth Matters*, Columbia Earth Institute, Spring 2000. www.earthinstitute. columbia.edu.
17. Berger, *Beating the Heat*, p. 31.
18. Patrick J. Michaels, "Carbon Dioxide: A Satanic Gas?" Testimony before the Subcommittee on National Economic Growth, CATO, October 6, 1999. www.cato.org.
19. Gerald Urquhart et al., "Tropical Deforestation," *Earth Observatory*, NASA, 2001. www.nasa.gov.
20. Quoted in PBS, *What's Up with the Weather?*

Chapter 4: Signs of a Warming Planet
21. Quoted in Hanna Goss, "Rising Seas: Maryland Managers Pursue Higher Ground," *Coastal Services Magazine*, NOAA, March/April 2000. www.csc.noaa.gov.
22. Quoted in British Antarctic Survey (press release), "Satellite Spies on Doomed Antarctic Ice Shelf," March 19, 2002. www.antarctica.ac.uk.
23. Quoted in Eve Savory, "The Shrinking Polar Bears," *The National*, CBC Canada, July 1, 1999. www.tv.cbc.ca.
24. Quoted in Doug O'Harra, "As Alaska Thaws, Engineers Eye Strange New World," *Anchorage Daily News*, January 9, 2003, p. A-1. www.alaska.com.
25. Quoted in Ned Rozell, "Thawing Permafrost Threatens Alaska's Foundation," *Alaska Science Forum*, Geophysical Institute, January 23, 1997. www.gi.alaska.edu.
26. DeNeen L. Brown, "Waking the Dead, Rousing Taboo in Northwest Canada, Thawing Permafrost Is Unearthing Ancestral Graves," *National Association of Tribal Historic Preservation Officers*, October 17, 2001. www.nathpo.org.
27. Quoted in Gabrielle Walker, "Climate Change Scenario," *New Scientist*. n.d. www.newscientist.com.
28. World Wildlife Fund, "Global Warming & Atlantic Hurricanes," September 1999. www.worldwildlifefund.org.
29. Gagosian, "Triggering Abrupt Climate Change."

Chapter 5: Global Warming and the Future
30. Weier, "Global Warming."
31. Quoted in PBS, *What's Up with the Weather?*

32. Quoted in PBS, *What's Up with the Weather?*

33. Richard S. Lindzen, "Global Warming: The Origin and Nature of the Alleged Scientific Consensus," *CATO Review of Business & Government*, CATO, 1992, vol. 15, no. 2. www.cato.org.

34. Craig D. Idso and Keith E. Idso, "Elitist Leaders Out of Step with Scientific Reality," *Editorial Commentary*, Center for the Study of Carbon Dioxide and Global Change, February 2001. www.co2science.org.

35. Thomas Gale Moore, "Global Warming: Try It, You Might Like It," CATO *Dailys*, June 4, 1998. www.cato.org.

36. Quoted in PBS, *What's Up with the Weather?*

37. Quoted in Curtis Runyan, "Ocean Warming Studies Bolster Evidence of Human Hand in Climate Change," *World Watch*, July/August 2001, p. 10.

38. Quoted in PBS, *What's Up with the Weather?*

39. Weier, "Global Warming."

40. Firor, interview with the author.

41. Quoted in PBS, *What's Up with the Weather?*

42. Schneider, *Global Warming*, p. 36.

Chapter 6: A Cooler Earth

43. Quoted in PBS, *What's Up with the Weather?*

44. Moore, "Global Warming."

45. Berger, *Beating the Heat*, p. 81.

46. Quoted in PBS, *What's Up with the Weather?*

47. Union of Concerned Scientists, "Common Sense on Climate Change: Practical Solutions to Global Warming." n.d. www.ucsusa.org.

48. Quoted in PBS, *What's Up with the Weather?*

49. Royal Dutch/Shell Group of Companies, "Our Approach to Climate Change." n.d. www.shell.com.

50. Berger, *Beating the Heat*, pp. 86–87.

51. Patrick J. Michaels, "Abrupt Climate Noise," *National Review Online*, December 19, 2001. www.nationalreviewonline.com.

52. Patrick J. Michaels, Paul C. Knappenberger, and Robert E. Davis, "The Way of Warming," *Regulation Magazine*, CATO, Fall 2000, p. 14. www.cato.org.

53. Quoted in Andrew C. Revkin, "Who Cares About a Few Degrees?" *New York Times*, November 27, 1997. www.ny times.com.

Glossary

anthropogenic: Caused by humans.

atmosphere: The layer of mixed gases that surrounds the earth.

biomass energy: Energy that is created from organic waste.

carbon dioxide (CO$_2$): A gas that occurs naturally in the atmosphere, and is also produced during the decaying of plants or when fossil fuels are burned.

carbon sink: An area, such as a forest, that stores and traps carbon dioxide.

chlorofluorocarbons (CFCs): A family of chemicals developed for use in air conditioners and refrigerators, and also as coolants and aerosol propellants.

climate: The average, or normal, weather for a particular region over a period of years.

coral reef: A colorful ridge or mound made by colonies of tiny animals called polyps, found only in shallow regions of tropical oceans.

food chain: The hierarchy of plants and animals in which one serves as the food for the next in the chain.

fossil fuels: Fuels from natural substances, such as coal, petroleum, and natural gas.

geothermal energy: Energy produced by the internal heat of the earth.

glacier: A huge mass of ice that has been formed by melted snow, ice, and rock debris.

global warming: An increase in average global temperatures.

greenhouse effect: The natural process whereby gases in the atmosphere act like the glass in greenhouse, letting the sun's energy in, and trapping some of it to warm the earth.

greenhouse gases: Gases that trap the heat of the sun in the earth's atmosphere, producing the greenhouse effect. The two major greenhouse gases are carbon dioxide and water vapor; others include methane, ozone, chlorofluorocarbons, and nitrous oxide.

hydropower: The production of electricity by harnessing the power of flowing water.

ice sheets: Very large masses of ice that can be several miles thick (also called ice caps).

Little Ice Age: A cold period that lasted from the mid-1500s to the mid-1800s in Europe, North America, and Asia.

methane: A gas formed by the decomposition of organic waste; also a natural gas in the earth's atmosphere.

nitrous oxide: A greenhouse gas formed when nitrogen is combined with oxygen.

paleoclimatology: The study of ancient climates.

permafrost: Permanently frozen ground that is located in cold climates.

photosynthesis: The process by which plants convert sunlight into food energy.

photovoltaic: Technology for converting sunlight into electricity.

phytoplankton: Microscopic plants found in water that serve as the basis of the food chain.

Pleistocene epoch: The Ice Age, which started nearly 2 million years ago and ended about 13,000 B.C.

renewable resources: Resources such as wind that can be replenished, or that cannot be used up.

sinkhole: A visible depression in the earth's surface that is often caused by the collapse of rock or by permafrost.

varve: Layers of sediment deposited in a body of water during one year.

water vapor: Water that is present in the atmosphere; the most plentiful greenhouse gas.

weather: The specific condition of the atmosphere at a particular place and time, measured using such terms as wind, temperature, humidity, atmospheric pressure, cloudiness, and precipitation.

wetlands: A natural habitat for many plants, birds, and wildlife in which the ground is flooded with water for most or all of the year.

zooxanthellae: Tiny algae cells that live inside coral polyps and give them their vivid colors.

For Further Reading

Books

Jean F. Blashfield and Wallace B. Black, *Global Warming*. Chicago: Childrens Press, 1991. Covers such topics as climate change, global warming, and predictions for the future.

Ron Fridell, *Global Warming*. New York: Franklin Watts, 2002. Discusses various theories on the causes and solutions of global warming, including some scientific predictions for the future.

Laurence Pringle, *Global Warming: The Threat of Earth's Changing Climate*. New York: SeaStar Books, 2001. Examines possible consequences of global warming, and the ways it might be slowed down. Illustrated with photographs, drawings, and charts.

Periodicals

Jan Gilbreath, "Ocean Temperatures, Global Warming Linked," *United Press International (UPI)*, March 23, 2000.

Alexandra Hanson-Harding, "Global Warming: What Is Global Warming and How Can We Slow It?" *Junior Scholastic*, April 8, 2002.

Patricia Janes, "Tales from the Ice," *Science World*, November 12, 2001.

John O'Brien, "Planetary Blanket," *Blast Off* (Macquarie Centre, Australia), September 2001.

Lidia Wasowicz, "Warming Wipes Out Coral Reef Population, *United Press International (UPI)*, May 10, 2000.

Alexandra Witze, "Arctic Adventure May Shed New Light on Climate Change," *Dallas Morning News*, May 13, 2002.

Websites

Environmental Protection Agency (EPA) Kids Site (www.
epa.gov). Especially developed for young people, this site
discusses the greenhouse effect, climate, weather, and the causes
of global warming.

National Renewable Energy Laboratory (www.nrel.gov). A
good site to learn about what renewable energy is, how it is
created, and how it is used.

Study Works! Online (www.studyworksonline.com). Designed
to help kids succeed in math and science. Includes a special
section on global warming.

**University Corporation for Atmospheric Research *Win-
dows to the Universe*** (www.windows.ucar.edu). A fun site
that helps kids explore issues related to Earth and space.

Works Consulted

Books

John J. Berger, *Beating the Heat: Why and How We Must Combat Global Warming.* Berkeley, CA: Berkeley Hills Books, 2000. Begins with a "what if?" chapter in which the author examines what may happen to the world if global warming is not stopped; follows with an explanation of heat-trapping gases, myths about global warming, and a list of better energy sources.

Stephen H. Schneider, *Global Warming: Are We Entering the Greenhouse Century?,* San Francisco: Sierra Club Books, 1989. Examines the causes and effects of worldwide climate change and provides a wealth of facts about global warming, including controversy surrounding it.

Periodicals

Curtis Runyan, "Ocean Warming Studies Bolster Evidence of Human Hand in Climate Change," *World Watch*, July/August 2001.

Gabrielle Walker, "Wild Weather," *New Scientist*, September 16, 2000.

Internet Sources

British Antarctic Survey (press release), "Satellite Spies on Doomed Antarctic Ice Shelf," March 19, 2002. www.antarctica.ac.uk.

Wallace S. Broecker, Lamont-Doherty Earth Observatory, Columbia University. www.ldeo.columbia.edu.

DeNeen L. Brown, "Waking the Dead, Rousing Taboo in Northwest Canada, Thawing Permafrost Is Unearthing Ancestral Graves," *National Association of Tribal Historic Preservation Officers,*

October 17, 2001. www.nathpo.org.

Gale Christianson, "From Benevolence to Menace: An Historian's Biography of Global Warming," *Earth Matters*, Columbia Earth Institute, Spring 2000. www.earthinstitute.columbia.edu.

CNN, "Deciphering the Ice," *America's Best Society and Culture*, 2001. www.cnn.com.

Robert B. Gagosian, "Triggering Abrupt Climate Change: Can Global Warming Cause an 'Ice Age'?," *What's New?*, Woods Hole Oceanographic Institute. www.whoi.edu.

Hanna Goss, "Rising Seas: Maryland Managers Pursue Higher Ground," *Coastal Services Magazine*, NOAA, March/April 2000. www.csc.noaa.gov.

William Hutton, "Scientists, in Their Own Words," *The Hutton Commentaries*, February 1, 2001. www.huttoncommentaries. com.

Craig D. Idso and Keith E. Idso, "Elitist Leaders Out of Step with Scientific Reality," *Editorial Commentary*, Center for the Study of Carbon Dioxide and Global Change, February 2001. www.co2science.org.

Richard S. Lindzen, "Global Warming: The Origin and Nature of the Alleged Scientific Consensus," *CATO Review of Business & Government*, CATO, 1992, vol. 15, no. 2. www.cato.org.

Patrick J. Michaels, "Abrupt Climate Noise," *National Review Online*, December 19, 2001. www.nationalreviewonline.com.

———, "Carbon Dioxide: A Satanic Gas?" Testimony before the Subcommittee on National Economic Growth, CATO, October 6, 1999. www.cato.org.

Patrick J. Michaels, Paul C. Knappenberger, and Robert E. Davis, "The Way of Warming," *Regulation Magazine*, CATO, Fall 2000. www.cato.org.

Thomas Gale Moore, "Do Climate Changes Mean Anything?" *World Climate Report Essays*, August 31, 1998. www.stan ford.edu.

———, "Global Warming: Try It, You Might Like It," CATO *Dailys*, June 4, 1998. www.cato.org.

NASA, "About the Terra Spacecraft," *Terra: The Earth Observing System (EOS) Flagship.* http://terra.nasa.gov.

National Oceanic and Atmospheric Administration (NOAA), *Paleoclimatology Program.* www.ngdc.noaa.gov.

Doug O'Harra, "As Alaska Thaws, Engineers Eye Strange New World," *Anchorage Daily News*, January 9, 2003. www.alaska. com.

PBS, *What's Up with the Weather?* December 30, 1999. www.pbs.org.

Andrew C. Revkin, "Who Cares About a Few Degrees?" *New York Times*, November 27, 1997. www.nytimes.com.

Royal Dutch/Shell Group of Companies, "Our Approach to Climate Change." n.d. www.shell.com.

Ned Rozell, "Thawing Permafrost Threatens Alaska's Foundation," *Alaska Science Forum*, Geophysical Institute, January 23, 1997. www.gi.alaska.edu.

Eve Savory, "The Shrinking Polar Bears," *The National*, CBC Canada, July 1, 1999. www.tv.cbc.ca.

Union of Concerned Scientists, "Common Sense on Climate Change: Practical Solutions to Global Warming." n.d. www. ucsusa.org.

Gerald Urquhart et al., "Tropical Deforestation," *Earth Observatory*, NASA, 2001. www.nasa.gov.

Gabrielle Walker, "Climate Change Scenario," *New Scientist*. n.d. www. newscientist.com.

John Weier, "Global Warming," NASA, April 8, 2002. www. nasa.gov.

World Wildlife Fund, "Global Warming & Atlantic Hurricanes," September 1999. www.worldwildlifefund.org.

Index

Picture Credits

Cover photo: NASA/Photo Researchers, Inc.
AP/Wide World Photos, 10, 23, 59, 64, 70, 76, 80, 88
© Corel Corporation, 26, 73
Tony Craddock/Photo Researchers, Inc., 69
Paul Fletcher/Photo Researchers, Inc., 75
© Stephen Frink/CORBIS, 57
© Raymond Gehman/CORBIS, 56
Hulton/Archive by Getty Images, 42, 46
© Hulton-Deutsch Collection/CORBIS, 35
Chris Jouan, 12, 15, 18, 41, 48, 52, 91
© Steve Kaufman/CORBIS, 62
© Jacques Langevin/CORBIS SYGMA, 78
Debbie Larson, NWS, International Activities, National Oceanic and
     Atmospheric Administration/ Department of Commerce, 66
Dr. James P. Mcvey, NOAA Sea Grant Program/National Oceanic and
     Atmospheric Administration/ Department of Commerce, 32
© PhotoDisc, 29, 49, 83, 93
Photo Researchers, Inc., 38
© Joseph Sohm; ChromoSohm Inc./CORBIS, 86
Sinclair Stammers/Photo Researchers, Inc., 31

About the Author

Peggy J. Parks holds a bachelor of science degree from Aquinas College in Grand Rapids, Michigan, where she graduated magna cum laude. She is a freelance writer and author who has written numerous titles for The Gale Group, including titles in the Lucent Books series Careers for the 21st Century, the Blackbirch Press series Giants of Science and Nations in Conflict, and the KidHaven Press series Exploring Careers, Our Environment, Daily Life, and Science Libraries. She was previously the profile writer for *Grand Rapids: The City That Works*, produced by Towery Publications. Parks lives in Muskegon, Michigan, a town that she says inspires her writing because of its location on the shores of Lake Michigan.